"Nearly 40 years ago, I took up a hobby: tracing my
eration fan chart. Jeanne Chevalier's name appeare
among some 1,024 others. Going over the pages of Lynne's book, I have found no longer just a name, but a real-life person, a woman I have come to know a little more through the dark veils of the thirty decades since she left this world. I dare say I have almost come to love her, as I did her descendants, my grandmothers."

~ *Father C. Peter Dumont*

"As an eighth great-granddaughter of Jeanne Chevalier, I read this history and began to reflect on the legacy she left. Until Lynne's book, I had no idea I was descended from a *Fille du Roi*. I did know that my ancestors came from France and was always proud of that fact.

"As a child brought up in a Franco-American household, I heard stories of my aunts, uncles, grandparents and great grandparents told to me by my mother and father. How they traveled down from Canada to settle in Nashua, NH. They were not so different from Jeanne as they pioneered into a new country. They became successful and raised children with a set of values that I believe is Jeanne's legacy. To tell each and every one of their stories would be a paramount undertaking. To parallel their lives to Jeanne's and recount their successes, perils, and sorrows gives her life great meaning.

"I cherish this gift that Lynne has given to us, Jeanne's family. I will share it with my children and someday my grandchildren. And if by chance I am asked about my ancestry, I will proudly share the story of Jeanne. Thank you Lynne."

~ *Susan Littlefield*

Jeanne Chevalier, Fille du Roi
Her Story

By Lynne C. Levesque

This book was originally printed at Harvard Book Store, Cambridge Massachusetts USA.

Layout and design by Caitlin Bechtel.
Cover photo of Coutances, France is by the author.
Author's photo by Carla M. Levesque.

ISBN 978-0-9979516-0-8

Sp

Shadow Press
27 Chelmsford Road
Rochester, NY 14618 USA

This book is dedicated to the present and future descendants of Jeanne Marguerite Chevalier, especially Cyrus, Maron, Max, Raina, Riley, Zoe and now Alexandra Louise. May you find inspiration from her story and the deep roots she represents.

Table of Contents

Map of Normandy

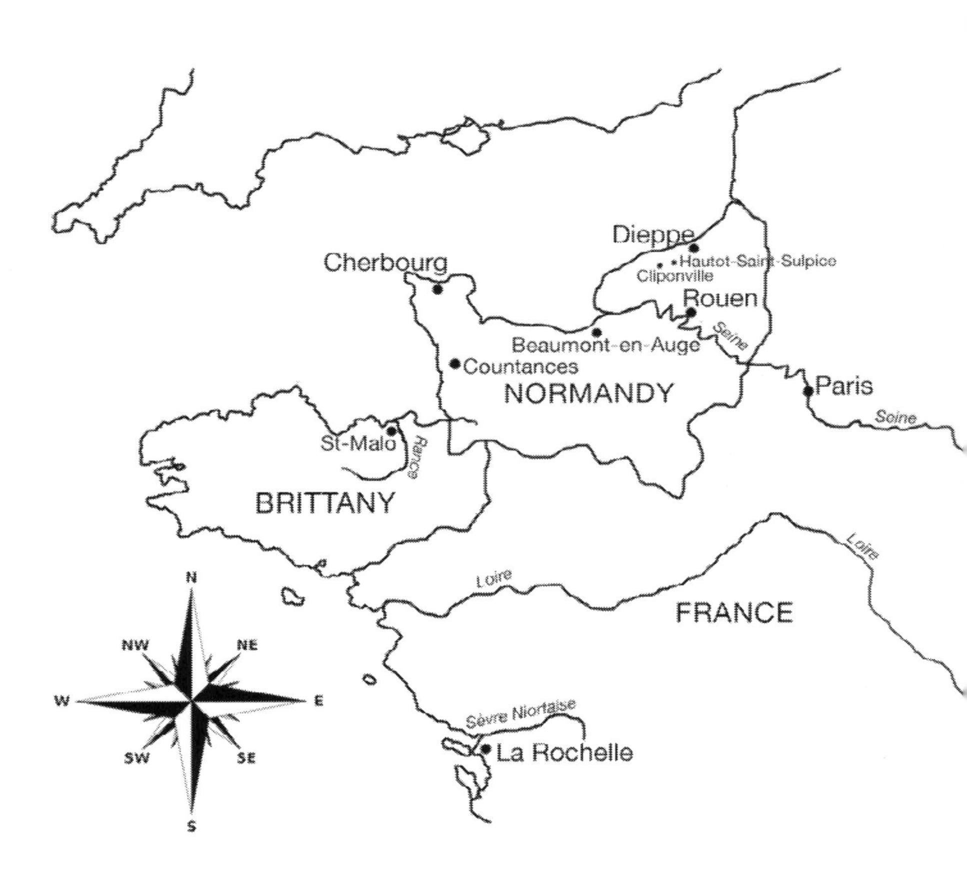

Map of 17th Century Quebec

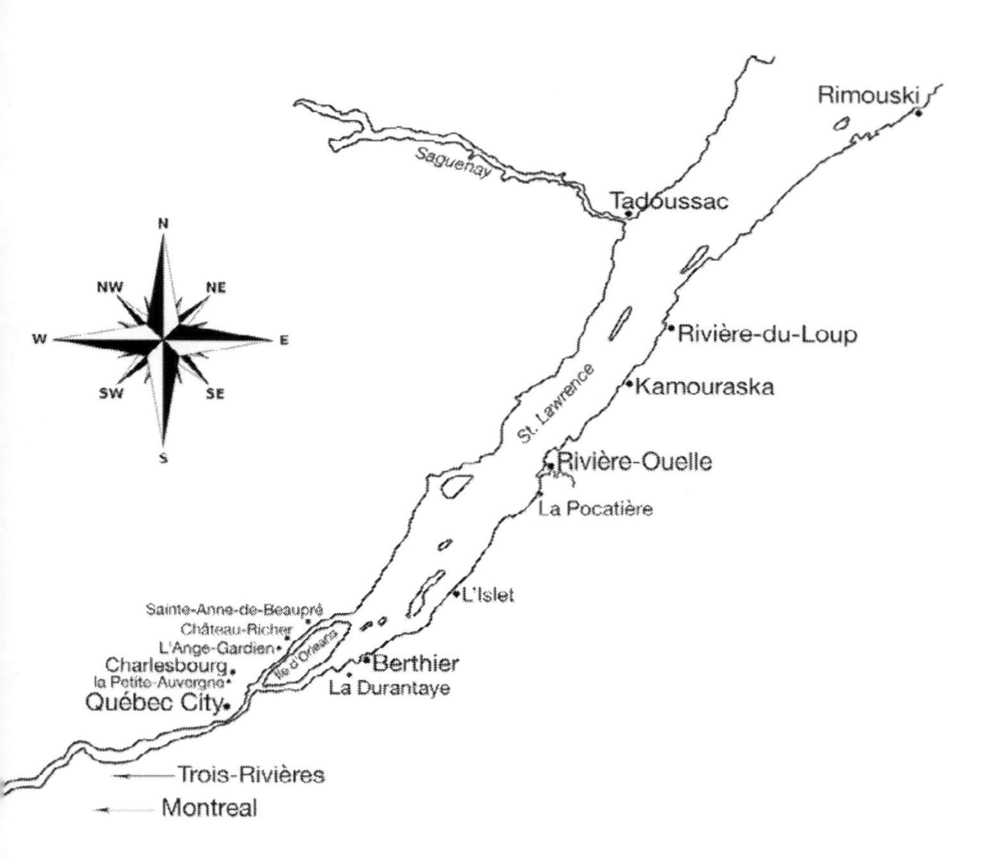

Lynne's Link To Jeanne

Jeanne Chevalier to Lynne C. Levesque

Jean-Alexandre (Jean or Jacques) Chevalier m. Marguerite Scorban (Scorinan)
Abt 1642 Normandie, France

Robert Lévesque m. **Jeanne Chevalier**
22 April 1679, L'Ange-Gardien, Québec

François-Robert Lévesque m. M-Charlotte Aubert
7 November 1701, Rivière-Ouelle, Kamouraska, PQ

Jean-Baptiste Lévesque m. M-Josephte Bérubé
18 July 1736, Rivière-Ouelle, Kamouraska, PQ

Charles Lévesque m. Catherine Beaulieu-Hudon
17 January 1769, Rivière-Ouelle, Kamouraska, PQ

Germain Lévesque m. Geneviève Charrois
13 October 1794, St. Roch-des-Aulnaies, PQ

Joseph Lévesque m. Léocadie Lavoie
19 January 1841, Église St. Louis, Kamouraska, PQ

Martial Lévesque m. Thècle Dufour
9 February 1864, St. Denis de-la-Bouteillerie, PQ

Joseph M. Levesque m. Clara April
7 January 1890, Nashua, New Hampshire

Treffle George Levesque m. Marie Brodeur
3 September 1917, Nashua New Hampshire

J. Gerard Levesque m. Judith Hallstrom
27 December 1943, Nashua, New Hampshire

Lynne C. Levesque

Introduction to Jeanne's History

Over the course of eleven years, from 1663 through 1673, 770 young women left France. With the support of the Sun King, Louis XIV, they braved the many weeks of the voyage across the Atlantic Ocean to Canada. They were on a mission, sent by the King to marry the soldiers, adventurers, farmers, and other men who wanted to settle in New France. Encouraged by the King's offer of supplies and a dowry, these courageous young women, most of them orphans, would not only marry and bear an average of seven children each, thus quickly expanding the population of the colony within a few short years. These "founding mothers" would also give birth to a unique heritage for hundreds of thousands of descendants in Canada and the United States.

My ancestor, my eighth great grandmother, Jeanne Marguerite Chevalier, was one of these pioneering women, who became known as the "Daughters of the King," or *Filles du Roi.* Twenty-eight years after she was baptized in St. Nicolas Church in the cathedral town of Coutances in Lower Normandy on June 8, 1643, she chose to find a new future and leave France forever. Arriving in Quebec City in the summer of 1671, roughly two months after she left from the port of Dieppe in northern France, this remarkable woman went on to marry and then outlive three husbands and survive the births of nine children and the deaths of six of them.

Impoverished by her first husband, she worked with the second to establish one of the largest landholdings in the region, one that was sufficient to leave her surviving children well settled with land, homes and livestock, although apparently not without some tensions. And her marriage with the third one brought an almost fairy tale ending to her life. When she died at the age of 73, in November 1716, forty-five years after her arrival in Quebec, she left three sons, 32 grandchildren, and a long line of descendants. Those descendants include René Lévesque, the founder of the *Parti Québécois* and the 23rd Premier of Quebec, the author Jack Kerouac, and my father Gerard Joseph Levesque.

Like many of these women and the men they were to marry, Jeanne could neither read nor write. There are no journals, no diaries, and no stories about them handed down through the family from so many ages ago. Nevertheless, her story must be told—beyond the few short paragraphs to which it has to date been relegated. Jeanne Marguerite Chevalier was an extraordinary woman, as were most of the other *Filles du Roi*. She faced an incredible number of challenges and dangers and endured many sorrows. Through it all, she was able to create a life for herself and her children that she could never have imagined if she had stayed in France.

In order to give Jeanne the voice and recognition she deserves, I have spent many, many hours in archives and libraries in the United States, Quebec and France as well as on the Internet. I have talked, in person or via email, with several authors as well as descendants of Jeanne's second and third husbands. I have read the books of historians, particularly Leslie Choquette, Silvio Dumas, Cole Harris, Peter Gagné, Paul-Henri Hudon, Alain Laberge, Gustave Lanctôt, Yves Landry, Renaud Lévesque, Ulric Lévesque, Eric Mardoc, Peter Moogk, Jan Noel, Aimie Runyan, and Marcel Trudel, among others.

In addition, because of the growing interest in the *Filles du Roi* among French Canadians, the vast majority of whom have more than one of these remarkable women as ancestors, I have benefited from many fictional accounts, based on real or imaginary *Filles du Roi*. I have also dug up old history books to gain a better understanding of French and Quebec history at the time. Parts of Jeanne's story rely heavily on the work of all these authors and others because they provide valuable details about life in France and New France in the 17th century. Many also contain very useful transcriptions of documents written in Old French. (A full bibliography and list of acknowledgements are included at the end of this book.)

The result of all this research is this book, the first of its kind in English—to the best of my knowledge. It is not a novel but a history of her life. The pictures, unless otherwise indicated, are from my journey to uncover Jeanne's story.

Jeanne's is a story full of facts, mysteries, and unknowns. It's a story of endings and new beginnings. And it's a story of much courage, stamina, will, and many choices. This first edition, written 300 years after Jeanne's death by her 8th great granddaughter, provides—as much as is possible—the details of those endings, beginnings and choices, all set in the context of the times and places where she lived.

Part One: Leaving France 1643–1671 (chapters 1 and 2) describes Jeanne's life through her departure from France and gives background on the *Filles du Roi* program, as well.

Part Two: New France 1671–1679 (chapters 3–5) provides background on the New France that became Jeanne's home in 1671 and details her life through the death of her first husband.

Part Three: Rivière-Ouelle 1679–1699 (chapters 6–10) covers the next twenty years of Jeanne's life.

Part Four: **Rivière-Ouelle 1699–1716** (chapters 11–13) describes the events that occurred after the death of her second husband, through her own death.

Part Five: Legacies (chapters 14 and 15) defines her legacy and the legacy of her three husbands.

The **Conclusion** offers some perspectives on Jeanne's life and the contribution she and the other *Filles du Roi* (and their husbands) made to Quebec.

Finally, the **Epilogue** describes some of the challenges I have encountered in this journey and my next steps to uncover more of Jeanne's story. It also includes a request to readers for feedback and further information to help me in my continued research into the life of this remarkable woman.

The **Appendices** provide readers with additional resources, including a Cast of Characters and Glossary.

Message to Readers: Please note that because of the nuances of the French language that make exact translation difficult, I have often used French terms which I have highlighted in italics, at their first appearance. At the back of the book, the Glossary provides more detailed definitions of these frequently used French terms.

Part One

Leaving France:

Jeanne's life through her departure from France (1643–1671)
and background on the *Filles du Roi* program.

1

Jeanne's France

On Monday morning, January 30, 1713, Jeanne Marguerite Chevalier sat in her room in Rivière-Ouelle, far to the east of Quebec City along the southern shore of the St. Lawrence River, and dictated her will, an unusual action for women—and men—at the time. The temperature outside would have been well below zero and the ground would have been frozen and covered with layers of snow for months. Her sons had promised to build a brick stove in her bedroom and supply her with plenty of wood so undoubtedly there was a good fire burning to keep the room warm.

Jeanne was 69 years old and was now living in the house that had been her home for so many years with her second husband, Robert Lévesque, and, for a short time, with her third husband as well. The home now belonged to her second son with Robert, as a result of the agreement reached with all three of her sons in July, 1705.

Was she looking out the window at the view on the Ouelle River that snaked its way from the distant hills in the south down through the village to empty into the St. Lawrence River? Or was she instead concentrating on the men in the room, the Notary Etienne Janneau and the other two men who would be witnessing her will?

Over the next couple of hours she would dictate her wishes to Janneau who wrote them down, in front of the witnesses. The will followed a format prescribed at the time and included all the sentences that have become well known about the state of her mind and soul. Jeanne had Janneau describe the provisions for her funeral, burial, and the services to be held after her death and then list her bequests. These included masses to be said for her soul and the souls of her second husband and the deceased children of her first marriage. She asked for masses to be said in eight different churches. She acknowledged one dear friend. She made a not insignificant bequest to only one living relative. She did not mention either her first or third husband.

Janneau then read back to her what he had written, a routine procedure at the time since she could neither read nor write. She asked for six words to be deleted as incorrect or unnecessary. They were crossed out or corrected in the original copy. Then the will was signed by Janneau and the two witnesses. Jeanne lived for nearly four more years before the will went into effect, apparently leading an active life that included possibly attending a baptism in the village of L'Ange-Gardien on the north shore of the St. Lawrence where she had once had a home.

After the will was signed and the men had left, did Jeanne spend any time reflecting on her life and wondering what it would have been like if she had not moved to Quebec so long ago and instead had remained in France? Did she think back to that day in June, 1671, over forty years earlier, when at the age of twenty-eight, she had boarded a ship in Dieppe harbor and left France forever? Although single and orphaned, she had not been alone on the ship since there were one hundred other women, all of them *Filles du Roi,* also bound for Quebec that year, most of them, like Jeanne, never to return.

Seventeenth Century France

Some significant events that provide context for the France that Jeanne was leaving in 1671 include:

911	Norse chieftain Rollo obtains Normandy after signing treaty with French king
1066	William, Duke of Normandy, becomes king of England after victory at battle of Hastings
1204	Normandy annexed to France
1337-1453	Hundred Years War between England and France
1450	Development of the printing press and moveable type
1517	Martin Luther nailed the 97 theses to the door of the church in Wittenburg
1541-1549	Jean Calvin in Geneva spearheaded the foundation of the Protestant church in France
1562-1598	Religious wars in France between Catholics and French Huguenots (French Protestants)
1598	Edict of Nantes proclaimed
1611	King James Bible published in England
1616	Death of William Shakespeare
1631	First French newspaper published
1633	Trial of Galileo for his revelation that the earth was not the center of the universe.
1638	Louis XIV was born in St. Germain-en-Laye, France
1639	Economic disasters in France; Nu-Pieds revolt in Normandy
1642	Death of Galileo, but scientific revolution had begun Rembrandt painted "The Night Watchmen"
1643	Death of Louis XIII; his son Louis XIV became King. Jeanne Marguerite Chevalier born in Coutances, Lower Normandy, France
1648	The Thirty Years War in Europe ended
1648	The uprising of many French nobles, known as *La Fronde*, erupted and died out eight years later.
1661 ff	Crisis and chaos in France: Beginning of personal rule of Louis XIV, government reorganization and consolidation of power; France plagued by bad weather, famine and epidemics
1663	New France became a colony of the French crown
1666	Vermeer painted "The Girl with a Pearl Earring"
1667	John Milton published *Paradise Lost*

***

The France Jeanne was leaving was not the most promising place for a young woman of humble origins. The years that preceded and immediately followed her birth in 1643 marked a time, for Europe at least, of exploration and expansion politically, geographically as well as in the arts and sciences. Spanish, Dutch, Portuguese, British, and French navigators and merchants were discovering new lands and finding new peoples in Africa, Asia and the Americas, in their search for treasure and routes to the Far East. On the heels of the Reformation and Renaissance, it was also a time of rebellion, religious turmoil, civil conflict, consolidation of power by monarchs, and seemingly endless war. And for many, it was a time of economic distress.

Made up of a number of semi-autonomous states, with a jumble of laws, customs, weights and measures, France had 20 million inhabitants at the time and a land mass of over 200,000 square miles. Paris was the largest city in Christendom, closely rivaled by London. The French spoken in Paris was not the language of the realm. Multiple dialects and competing languages made communication and ruling a challenge.

The population in this 17th century France fell into several economic categories. At the top were the King, his court, and the clergy. Next were nobles, those who had received their titles either because of service to the crown, by inheritance, or more recently, by purchase. Below the nobles fell the lesser nobility, or "petite noblesse," made up of a growing number of nobles who generally had fallen on hard times or, conversely, those working their way up to higher echelons. Estate administrators, merchants, notaries, shopkeepers, and lawyers, most of whom usually lived in larger towns and cities, made up a middle class, the "*bourgeoisie*," with a wide range of economic circumstances, depending on their occupation and the amount of land they owned. Artisans, such as carpenters, masons, and others skilled in non-agricultural occupations, all with varying levels of success, might work in towns or as itinerants, moving from job to job, town to town.

They made up another class, the "most important citizens," according to one historian.

At the lowest end of the societal spectrum lived the peasants. Throughout the 17th century, life for the lower classes, who made up the greatest proportion of the population, was a constant, seemingly hopeless struggle. In addition to disasters caused by weather, famine, and epidemics, they were subjected to increasing taxes to support the extravagant spending of Louis XIII and those kings who preceded and followed him. Tithes and rents to the church and their landlord only added to their burden, as did the sequestration of troops resulting from wars with France's neighbors.

Into this world Jeanne Marguerite Chevalier was born, three weeks after four-year-old Louis XIV was crowned King of France on the premature death of his father, Louis XIII. She was baptized on June 8, 1643 in the small cathedral town of Coutances, 330 kilometers from Paris, at the lower end of the Cotentin Peninsula in what was to be called "Lower Normandy." Situated at the top of a rocky promontory, Coutances is located just to the northeast of Mont St. Michel and not far from the university town of Caen where William the Conqueror and his wife Mathilda are buried.

The history of Coutances predates Roman times. Originally established as the capital of a Gaullish tribe in the first century BC, it was named "Constantia" by the Romans around 300 AD. It became Christian at the beginning of the 5th century. In 866 the town was invaded and then settled by Scandinavian invaders, known as "Normans." In 911 Rollo, the Norman chieftain, signed a treaty with the King of France, which gave Rollo all of what is now Normandy. The following centuries witnessed a great deal of growth in Normandy, both economically and politically. Norman dukes grew to be very powerful, sometimes rivaling the King of France.

In 1066 one of those dukes, William, known as the "Bastard" because of his origin, sailed to England from the shores of Normandy to claim his right to the English throne and earn the title "William the Conqueror." His successors ruled both England and Normandy until

1204 when French King Philip II recaptured Normandy and officially annexed it to France. Normandy remained French except for the three decades during the Hundred Year's war from 1418 until 1449 when it was under English rule. As a result of charters which recognized Norman rights and privileges, however, Normandy retained a great deal of freedom and autonomy until Louis XIV started to take them away as he consolidated his power.

Over the centuries Coutances had been ravaged and rebuilt several times. During their 15th century occupancy, the English destroyed many buildings in Coutances, including its walls and a chateau which were never rebuilt. Later, in the fighting between the Huguenots and the Catholics, Protestant forces invaded Coutances in 1562, murdered many inhabitants, destroyed statues in the cathedral, and returned to sack the town several times until 1598.

Decades later, during the *Nu-Pieds* revolt, peasants in Normandy protested the salt tax which continued to increase and threaten their livelihood. The revolt left its scars on Coutances, with gallows erected in the square facing the cathedral to punish leaders. Heavy fines were also levied against the town. Suppressing the revolt was one of Louis XIII's last acts before he died.

Along the narrow, winding streets that still lead to the top of the promontory are old homes and shops that could have existed when Jeanne lived there—or at least their foundations might have been there. Coutances hosted a German detachment in its Town Hall and was relatively untouched during the Second World War until the Allies arrived on June 6, 1944. When fires ignited by incendiary bombs died out and the smoke cleared, 60% of Coutances was destroyed. Recovery of the city began after the Americans took possession of the town in late July, 1944. Much of Coutances has been rebuilt since then, but fortunately it has retained much of its medieval feel and reflects some of the legacy of earlier centuries.

When Jeanne was born, Coutances was a thriving market town, with a population of approximately 7,000 people and an active middle class, its *bourgeoisie*, made up of merchants, shopkeepers, and successful artisans. The textile and printing industries in particular were flourishing. Coutances was one of a few French cities with a public water supply, thanks to 13th century aqueducts. Everyday life, however, was not much different from the rest of France. The streets were littered with food, trash and human and animal sewage. Roads were often muddy and full of ruts. Life was noisy, dirty, smelly and tough. Knowledge about germs and bodily hygiene was still almost non-existent. Most people still believed that bathing, particularly in warm water, caused the spread of disease.

In addition to its bustling marketplace, Coutances was a religious center. The Gothic cathedral which still dominates the countryside and defines the skyline of Coutances was begun in the 13th century and enlarged over the years. There were also two parish churches, St. Pierre and St. Nicolas, several convents and a seminary founded in 1650, seven years after Jeanne was born, to educate priests. The old Ursuline convent built in the 17th century has been replaced with a market space. Half way down the southern slope of the hill, however, the *Hôtel-Dieu*, founded by the Augustinian nuns in 1209 as a convent, orphanage and hospital, still serves the town as a hospital, but is now graced with the local railroad station as its neighbor.

St. Nicholas Church

Of the two parish churches, both of which are still standing, St. Pierre more closely resembles the cathedral, with its tall spire, gothic exterior and ornate interior. It remains an active church although with a limited schedule of masses. To the east of the cathedral, sits St. Nicolas, a slightly older and more somber church whose architecture is a mix of styles, reflecting five centuries of modifications. Its interior today is much less ornate than either St. Pierre or the cathedral. It is no longer a working church but is instead now used for expositions and other special events. In Jeanne's time, however, St. Nicolas served the eastern half of Coutances, possibly the less wealthy part of the city. Its parish boundaries extended down to an older neighborhood, *Les Piliers,* located at the base of the hill's northern slope.

It is in St. Nicolas that Jeanne was baptized on June 8, 1643, and possibly in *Les Piliers* where she was born.

Other than a one-line entry registering her baptism and listing Guillemette LeBreton as her godmother, little else is certain about Jeanne's life in France. Jeanne's baptismal record does not list the names of her parents, a not uncommon situation in the St. Nicolas registers at the time. Godparents were usually family members, but nothing has been found to determine what relation, if any, her godmother had to the family. Several other children with the same family name are listed as having been born around that time in Coutances. Although the names of parents are also missing on these records as well, it's possible Jeanne had brothers or sisters.

The names of Jeanne's parents, particularly her mother's, on Jeanne's subsequent marriage contracts and other documents in Quebec provide no help in solving the mystery of Jeanne's years in France since there are several different variations of their names. Her father's name could have been Jacques or Jean-Jacques or Jean Alexandre, but always "le Chevalier" or "Chevalier." Her mother's first name was consistently "Marguerite." Her last name, however, is confusing: *Scormand*, *Scormian*, *Scorban*, *Romian*, and even *Le Normand*, all of which can be attributed to misunderstanding of the spelling by the first recorder of the name or possibly to later transcriptions of poor handwriting. There was no way to correct any errors at the time since Jeanne presumably could not read or write, and apparently did not carry any identity papers.

While the name "Le Chevalier" or "Chevalier" is fairly common in both parishes in Coutances, the various last names of Jeanne's mother cannot be found in the registers. A careful search of the archives for Coutances has not uncovered any records for individuals with any of those variations—no dates of a marriage, or deaths, or records of any other family members. There are no *Scormands*, *Scormians*, *Scorbans*, or other variations in Coutances or even in surrounding communities. According to a French genealogist, these were not common names for the area.

One historian believes that Jeanne's mother's name was actually "Escoulant,"and that the various last names in Quebec were misspellings based on an incorrect interpretation of the pronunciation of the name. He has been able to track the transformation of the spelling of "Escoulant" to "Scormand" and other variations. Indeed, the name *Escoulant* and its variations of *Escoban* and *Escormant* were common names in Coutances, in St. Nicolas parish, both in the 17th century and later. Individuals with that name are prominently listed in histories of Coutances and did at one point belong to the noble class. Although it is possible that Jeanne's mother was a member of the Escoulant family and might have had some noble blood, as this historian claims, details in subsequent documents in Quebec seem to cast doubts on this possible heritage.

All of this lack of documentation has made piecing together Jeanne's life for the 28 years before she left Dieppe in June, 1671 quite problematic. There are many conceivable versions to her story, but they are all conjectures.

The years from 1643 to 1671 when Jeanne was growing up were difficult ones for most of France. Once the *Fronde* was settled with the rebellious nobles, some peace returned to the countryside. However, inhabitants were not free of troubles caused by the weather, famine, epidemics, and the continued fighting between Catholics and Protestants. Her family may or may not have been shielded from these disruptions in their home in Coutances.

Although the tragedies of Corneille and Racine, the fables of La Fontaine, the comedies of Molière, and the letters of Madame Sévigny were beginning to appear, Jeanne, who was not able to sign her name, would probably not have noticed. It is most likely that she had little schooling. Public schools did not exist at the time, and any existing schools were run by religious communities and were generally available only to those who could afford to pay. Such schools were usually confined to the male population. It is doubtful that Jeanne's parents, who could have been merchants or artisans, would have had the resources to pay for Jeanne's education, even if they had wanted to. Although Normandy had a higher rate of literacy than the rest of France, only approximately a third of the population could read or write. The proportion was much lower for women. Even those men or women who could sign their name usually did so rather crudely, indicating a somewhat rudimentary education.

From what is known, Jeanne was raised in a Catholic home. Since Jeanne was later identified as coming from an urban environment, it is probably safe to assume that home was within the town limits of Coutances, not in the countryside. In Coutances, she would have learned basic domestic skills. She would have had little opportunity to make any decisions on her own since women, whether as part of a noble, bourgeois, or peasant family, were under the control of their fathers and husbands. If a father died, a guardian, frequently a male relative, was put in charge of a young girl or woman since women were rarely allowed much independence. Respectable roles consisted primarily of mother, wife or member of a religious order, futures that generally required some sort of dowry. Young women from families of limited means had little or no prospects of a good dowry and were limited to living at home, engaging in domestic work, hiring themselves out to a local family with the resources to take in help, or working out in the fields before finding a husband. They could not travel on their own. Because of the economic requirements of starting a family, they tended to marry later in life, as did men.

When Jeanne left France in 1671, her father was deceased. He could have died at any point prior to her departure, possibly in the disastrous famine of 1661. Although her mother was still alive, at least until 1679, she may or may not have been able to take care of Jeanne on her own. In that case, Jeanne could have been raised by relatives or nuns at the *Hôtel-Dieu*, today's version of an orphanage. Without a dowry, she could have joined the convent as a lay nun or she could have become a servant in a noble family's home. The archivist in Coutances in 2011, in response to a question regarding what might have happened to Jeanne, had answered, "Perhaps she went to Paris to seek her fortune." She said this with a bit of disdain, reflecting the myth about the dubious character of the women who left for New France that has evolved over the years and in fact still exists!

Jeanne's family was not listed in the Coutances register for 1666. Therefore, the family must have moved—together as a family, as mother and daughter, or as daughter and family friend. Migrations from city to city were not frequent, but were not unknown. Of course, they could have moved to any number of different towns. However, her first marriage contract listed her parents as being "from St. Jacques parish in Dieppe." There is thus a strong possibility that they moved at some point from Coutances to Dieppe, located at the upper end of Normandy. They probably lived there long enough for Jeanne to be able to claim that her parents were "from Dieppe." It could even have been a move to be with extended family. There were indeed "le Chevaliers" in Dieppe in the 17th century, but no *Scorbans, Scormands* or *Escoulants.* Still, no traces of Jeanne in Dieppe have yet been uncovered, only the reference in the first marriage contract.

Somehow Jeanne and her family or other companions made the 240 kilometer, or approximately two week, journey from Coutances to Dieppe. Although there were carriages along the roads and even the possibility of arriving by fishing boat, most travel in the 17th century for all but the well-to-do was by foot along unpaved roads and paths. They would have had to stop at inns along the way and would have had to take a ferry to cross the Seine River that separated the lower half of Normandy from its upper half.

While it had a much larger population than Coutances, Dieppe was another thriving market town and was located on the English Channel, less than 200 kilometers northwest of Paris. Instead of textiles and publishing, Dieppe's fame came from its vibrant trading, fishing, and ivory industries and from its school of cartography. Merchants from the town played a major role in exploring and mapping North

Dieppe Château-Musée

America, through their support of maritime expeditions in the 16th century. Dieppe fisheries were said to make frequent deliveries of their products over direct roads to Paris. As a port city, Dieppe also served as a point of debarkation for many emigrants to Canada throughout the 17th century. And it still hosts a large, bustling and centuries-old Saturday market.

Like Coutances, Dieppe was one of a few cities in France with a public water system. Vestiges of some of the wells and fountains still exist; one, in fact, is a popular gathering place. The town does not have a long history dating back to Roman times, but Norsemen had arrived at the beginning of the 10th century. It too was a battleground during the Hundred Years War with England. Dieppe suffered greatly from an attack of the British and Dutch in 1694 and from a disastrous raid by the Allied forces on August 19, 1942 during World War II.

Dieppe had also been a walled city, although, with the passage of time and as the city grew, its walls had come down much later than those in Coutances. Two gates and mainly just traces remain today. Instead of being situated on the top of a promontory in the countryside like Coutances, Dieppe has grown up as a port between two limestone cliffs. And unlike Coutances, a 15th century chateau still sits on the western cliff, now the town's primary museum.

St. Jacques Church

Dieppe today has two parish churches and the remains of several convents, including the home of Augustinian nuns who left Dieppe for New France in 1639. All of the churches and convents are now closed or only used for special events, with one exception. St. Jacques, standing in the midst of old Dieppe and badly in need of repairs, still serves the Catholic population of Dieppe. It was there, in Dieppe, probably seated in St. Jacques Church, that Jeanne and her family must have heard about the King's plans for the *Filles du Roi*.

2

The King's Daughters Program of Louis XIV

The history of the "King's Daughters" or *Filles du Roi* program begins with young Louis XIV when he finally turned his attention to New France in 1663. Of course, he would then have learned that in fact, for over a century before him, France had been expanding its boundaries into North America.

At the turn of the 16th century, French fishermen from Normandy and Brittany had discovered fertile fishing waters off the coast of what would be called Newfoundland and Labrador. Shortly thereafter, Giovanni de Verrazano, a Florentine cartographer and navigator, funded by the French King Francis I and wealthy merchants from Dieppe and elsewhere, "discovered" the coast of America and sailed from Florida up to and beyond what is now New York City.

The first formal French claims to the land in North America came a decade later. A little over 100 years before Jeanne was born, Jacques Cartier had sailed from the port of St. Malo in Brittany, not very far from Jeanne's birthplace of Coutances, as part of French exploration initiatives. In 1534 he landed in what is now Eastern Canada, erected crosses, and claimed the land for Francis I—presumably much to the surprise of the members of the Canadian First Nation[1], the native population who met him on the banks of the St. Lawrence River, their home for many centuries.

Subsequent settlement in New France, however, was slow since

1 The terms "First Nation" and "Amerindians" are used interchangeably in this book and encompass the many different tribes of native peoples in Canada at the time.

the French kings were otherwise distracted by wars, religious turmoil and dynastic strife in Europe. Until Samuel Champlain founded Quebec in 1608, more than 70 years after Cartier's claim on behalf of the French king, the non-native population was still limited to fur traders, fishermen and a few merchants. At the time, the total French population in all of New France numbered less than 100 people. Without concerted French support, attempts at permanent settlement had failed. Only the trade in beaver furs kept the colony alive. In fact, in the de Ramezay Museum in Montreal, the beaver is credited with being the founder of New France!

In 1617, a hardy band of settlers arrived. Among them were Louis Hébert and his wife Marie Rollet who brought their three children with them from Normandy, becoming the first family to establish a home in Quebec. Neighbors were scarce, however. A decade after their arrival, there were only about 50 permanent settlers making their home in Quebec City, which was not much more than a cluster of hastily constructed buildings, with wharfs and sheds along the waterfront and a fort at the top of the cliff.

In order to spur development of the colony, French kings began to grant trading monopolies to various individuals and merchant associations in 1627 and charged them with developing the colony. The associations apparently failed to make a sustainable effort to colonize the land. Their work was made very difficult since the St. Lawrence, frozen for six months of the year, cut the colony off from the sea. Given the harsh climate, isolation, and rumors and realities about ever-changing relations with the Amerindians, it is not hard to understand why colonists might have been reluctant to emigrate from France. Only the most adventurous, those with dreams and determination, explorers like Jean Nicolet who had arrived in 1618 from Cherbourg, or those burning with religious zealousness would venture to make the voyage in those early years.

The Catholic Church did its best to aid in colonization. Jesuit priests had come to Quebec in 1625, as missionaries to the Amerindians. A group of Augustinian nuns from Dieppe arrived in Quebec in 1639, four years before Jeanne was born. They quickly established the *Hôtel-Dieu*, the first hospital in America north of Mexico, to minister to the souls and bodies of both the colonists and the natives.

That same year, Ursuline nuns, led by Marie de l'Incarnation, opened a convent in Quebec City as a school for young women. Three years later Jeanne Mance, a French missionary from Burgundy, helped found Montreal. The next year, the year Jeanne was born, three more Augustinian nuns arrived in Quebec City to help with the work at the hospital. The first church was built in Quebec City in 1647 on the site where the Cathedral of Notre-Dame now stands. The Catholic Church would continue to play a strong, important role in Quebec not only in helping to colonize New France. It also did its best to maintain a strict social order where divorce was infrequent and to keep detailed records of parish life—the latter a responsibility near and dear to the hearts of any historian!

Over the next several decades, despite the founding of Trois-Rivières in 1634 and Montreal (then called *Ville Marie)* eight years later, settlement in the colony had continued to be slow. The merchant associations were struggling to increase immigration. While men had been enticed to come to the colony with three-year contracts of engagement to work and then seek their fortune, they too often ended up returning to France at the end of their contracts instead of permanently settling down. Compounding the factors of the weather and unsettled relations with the First Nation peoples was the significantly unbalanced ratio of men to women. Attempts by individual merchants, family members, and the church to bring more women to New France had not been very successful. At one point, men outnumbered women by a ratio close to 10:1.

Back in France, Louis and his ministers had little time for the fledgling colony even though they had inherited plans from previous kings to expand into North America to make good on Cartier's claim and Champlain's efforts. They were still facing choices and challenges from external wars with Spain, the Netherlands, and Austria as well as from internal dissent posed by religious factions and rebellion from the nobles and from the peasants they lorded over. By 1663, however, the Peace of Westphalia and the Treaty of the Pyrenees had ended the wars within Europe. A semblance of calm had also arrived internally—at least for the time being. New initiatives were now required to realize the grand goals Louis had for France. For those in power, the new world appeared to provide the promise of opportunity. So 25-year-old Louis XIV decided to act.

In 1663, when the population in Quebec was still less than 3,000 inhabitants and when Jeanne was twenty years old, he sent over administrators to improve governance and troops to protect the fledgling French settlements along the banks of the St. Lawrence River. And starting in that year, Louis and his ministers established the *Filles du Roi* program, designed to encourage young, usually orphaned or impoverished, women to make the journey to New France, wed the explorers, soldiers, farmers, and traders, start families and thus expand the population.

It turns out, according to author Peter Gagné and others, that programs for bringing women to settle a colony in the New World were not really original to the French. Between 1619 and 1621, a private English company sent over 200 prospective brides for the settlers in Virginia. The brides-to-be lived with married couples until finding a suitable husband. Once married, their new husbands were responsible for repaying the cost of their brides' crossing with 120-150 pounds of their best tobacco.

The King of Spain similarly encouraged private adventurers in the 16th century to help colonize the Spanish West Indies. In this case, however, the emphasis was placed on married women and families. In fact, married men were forbidden from immigrating without their wives.

The French had also attempted to support the immigration of young unmarried women to New France. In the years prior to 1663, the cost of a woman's passage had been paid by merchants, family members, or the church. Future brides usually had some sort of family or other connection in the colony to encourage their decision to leave

France. These attempts prior to 1663, however, were not sufficient in numbers to accelerate growth of the colony.

Louis XIV's *Filles du Roi* program was different from previous attempts both in France and elsewhere. The young women, who had few if any family connections in the colony, were to be recruited and sent to New France by the King and his administrators. Unlike mail-order brides, they had no previous contact with possible husbands who were expected to pay their way. Indeed, under Louis' program, the women were to have the right to choose a husband when they arrived in New France.

In addition to their passage to New France, the King provided the young women with some basic clothing and the promise, upon marriage, of a dowry that varied from 50 to 100 livres or even higher, depending on a woman's status in society. The women also received several other necessary items, including a bonnet, taffeta handkerchief, ribbon, 100 needles, comb and hairbrush, white thread, a pair of stockings, a pair of gloves, a pair of scissors, two knives, 1,000 pins, 4 string laces for their bodices, and a small gift of money. They were expected to bring along personal property—their "trousseau"—which could include clothes, linen, keepsakes and other treasured possessions, all of which were stored in long wooden boxes, or *coffres*. The average value of these personal items, or "*biens,*" was 300 livres, but could range from 50 to 3000 livres.[2]

Coffres in Brussels

From 1663-1673, almost 800 young women, most of them between the ages of 16 and 40 years old, took up the call to serve the King and climbed aboard vessels that left either from the port at La

2 A unit of value used in France and New France at the time. See Glossary for further definition of the term.

Rochelle in western France or from the northern port of Dieppe. The majority of the women sailed from Dieppe, reached from other parts of France by boat or over land by carriage or on foot.

The women came from a variety of backgrounds and from many different locations in France. Most of them, in the early years of the program at least, were the orphaned daughters of minor artisans, laborers, servants, and sometimes lower, usually impoverished, nobility. The majority were from Paris or, like Jeanne, from towns and villages in Normandy or other parts of northwestern France. Roughly 25% of the *Filles du Roi* could sign their names. Jeanne was not one of them.

Given the lack of mass communication, widespread illiteracy, and the difficulties of seventeenth century travel, recruiters—primarily merchants and ship outfitters — focused their efforts around the ports of Dieppe and La Rochelle. Very few *Filles* came from the Cotentin Peninsula, where Jeanne was born. Therefore, it is doubtful she was still there when the program was announced and recruitment began.

Recruiters received a commission for every girl enrolled. The *Hôpital Général* and *La Pitié-Salpêtrière*, places in Paris that provided homes for abandoned children, orphaned girls, pregnant women, and even daughters of noble families that had fallen on hard times, were major sources of recruits. Approximately 50% of the *Filles du Roi* came from these institutions.

It seems that some number of young women just showed up at points of embarkation, perhaps lured by rumors about monetary gifts from the King. Apparently, despite the challenges of communication in 17th century France, the news of the program did eventually spread. There may even have been recruiting fliers posted in major cities. Somehow the program gained credibility since one-half of all *Filles du Roi* arrived in the later years of the program (1669-1673). Evidently, any stories coming back from New France must not have been all that grim.

In the first few years of the program, officials in Quebec voiced concerns that the young women being sent were not accustomed to or even physically capable of managing the heavy farm work, harsh winters, and isolation they would have to endure in New France. In response, Louis XIV's chief minister Jean-Baptiste Colbert, at Intendant Talon's urging, asked the Archbishop of Rouen in 1670 to spread the word throughout the many parishes in the nearby Norman countryside to find girls more accustomed to the hard rural life. "They must be healthy, strong," Talon had requested, "and in no way disgraced by nature and in no way repulsive on the outside!" According to the records of those women recruited in the next couple of years, the call for more recruits from rural areas was not very successful, since the majority of women continued to come from parishes in more urban areas.

That message went out in the churches around Rouen, including those in Dieppe, where Jeanne and her family could have heard the call. At 28, Jeanne was one of the older *Filles du Roi,* but the family must have decided it was still the best solution for Jeanne's future. For whatever reason, she had not yet found a husband. Perhaps no suitable husband or one to her liking had been found. Even if she had been born of a noble family of some means, there might not have been sufficient dowry for her to marry well or to enter a convent. Or perhaps she was a strong, determined young woman who did not need much encouragement to "volunteer" to leave.

The *Filles du Roi* program could thus have been an enticing alternative to the life she faced in France. There was, after all, a promised structure to the program, with a governess and priest to shepherd the young women on the ship, with financial support from the King, and with an organized welcome in Quebec. Jeanne was thus not going off to New France on her own. Her family could indeed send her off to the new colony with some well-founded hope for her future. They apparently were able to come up with a trousseau for Jeanne that was valued at 300 livres and included personal items that Jeanne would need or would not want to leave behind.

Whether Jeanne was recruited or just showed up at the docks in Dieppe is unknown. However, after saying goodbye to her mother and family, she would have joined other potential recruits as they went through a careful screening process. Recruiters had to make sure that the young women were not already married and were women of good standing in the Catholic Church. They required each to provide a birth certificate and affidavit from her priest confirming her freedom to marry. Unfortunately these documents seemed to have disappeared, destroyed in the 1694 bombardment of Dieppe, eaten by rats over the years, or perished during the wars of the 20th century. It's possible that the young women just brought them to New France, and they have been lost. Since no trace of any of these documents has ever been found in Quebec, it's more likely they remained in France.

The first contingent of 36 girls who arrived in Quebec on September 22, 1663 and the 734 who followed over the next ten years in increasing numbers were most certainly hardy women, even if many, like Jeanne, were not from rural backgrounds. They definitely must have heard some terrible stories of Canadian winters and Indian attacks, and they faced a potentially dangerous journey across the Atlantic Ocean. But for probably a variety of reasons, they decided to take a chance on a new life in Quebec.

Based on stories about other 17th century voyages, it's possible to recreate what those six weeks or longer on the ocean were like. Ships at the time were small, measuring 80-110 feet long and 25-30 feet wide, and crowded. There was no electricity, no running water, and no toilet facilities, except for a rude structure in the bow of the ship and buckets whose contents would be thrown overboard. Passengers were crowded into sleeping quarters like "sardines in a can," according to one voyager. Travelers shared the ship with animals being brought over to the colony or to be consumed on the voyage. The smells of animal dung, human waste, and the after effects of seasickness must

Replica of 17th century sailing ship [3]

3 Courtesy of Alain Testoris http://bit.ly/2eAooEx

have been intense. The sounds of tears, snoring, groaning, moaning, and other human noises only added to the roar of the sea and the creaking of the ship. Infestation of fleas, lice, mice and rats, lack of clean water, and no bathing options certainly made conditions worse.

Days were spent with prayers and masses on the main deck in good weather. Meals consisted of salted fish, dried meat and vegetables, soup, beans, and biscuits that today are called "hard tack." The animals on board might contribute to the offerings. Water was a treasured commodity and would have to be replaced with cider or "purified" with wine as the weeks went by. During storms, passengers would eat on their beds, or in worse cases, on the floor.

A great fear on board was fire. Stormy weather meant that meals were served cold because of this fear and the horrible damage a stove fire could cause on board. Candles or other lighting at night were thus forbidden, except for one light on deck. Nights were thus passed in almost total darkness unless a moon or stars lit up the sky.

In good weather, passengers were able to walk on the upper decks, watch whales and dolphins, and perhaps wonder about their decisions to leave France. When the lack of wind stalled the ship, they would pray for favorable weather. During storms, when the ship was rocking dangerously back and forth, side to side, everyone was required to stay inside and presumably to pray for survival. Portholes would be locked adding the lack of air to the list of many miseries. The threat of pirates and icebergs and possible death by scurvy or outbreaks of disease must have surely raised the anxiety level of most, if not all, passengers. In fact, 10% of passengers died before making land in New France

What sort of conversations did Jeanne and her fellow female companions have as they shared their miseries, worries, dreams, and revulsions at the probable catcalls and coarse language of the crew? Jeanne was part of one of the last contingents of women to be sent to New France so she must have heard stories, rumors, and words of advice that had trickled back from Quebec about what to expect there. Perhaps they even had lectures by the governess who shepherded each contingent of women from France to Quebec.

It's not too difficult to imagine those conversations on the ship coming over. The women would have been seated in their cramped quarters, sharing their stories, nervously fingering their rosaries. "I heard there are dangerous native people and wild animals. How are we going to protect ourselves from any attacks?" "Are we going to have to learn to shoot a rifle?" "What kind of man are you going to be looking for?" "How should we choose the right one?" "What sort of home should we expect to find?" "Will there be neighbors?"

After six weeks and sometimes longer at sea, depending on the weather, the currents and the winds that carried them to North America, the ships landed in Tadoussac on the north shore of the St. Lawrence. There they would pick up a guide who would navigate them up the river to Quebec City, another three or four days away. At news of a ship's final arrival in Quebec City, men were said to hurry to greet the passengers. Many were probably eager for female companionship. Orders from the King's administrator in Quebec, Intendant Jean Talon, requiring young men to find a bride soon after a ship's arrival or risk losing their hunting and fishing privileges most likely spurred them on as well. And perhaps the promise of the King's gifts upon marriage was an additional incentive. For whatever reason, the arrival of these women must have been a joy, at least for those seeking to stay in the colony, keep their freedom and the promise of a brighter future than in France, and still have a wife and family.

Records indicate that, upon arrival, the young women received more clothes to help them through the Canadian winter: a coat, woolen dress, coverings for their heads, and sheepskin gloves. Most of the women stayed in Quebec City with a governess from the trip continuing to watch carefully over them. About a quarter continued on up the river to Trois-Rivières and Montreal. It's not clear how those choices were made. Those who continued on might have actually been the more courageous given the frequency of attacks by the First Nation people further west of Quebec City.

In the early years of the program, many women in Quebec City were sheltered in dormitory-style housing in the home of the widow

Madame de la Peltrie, next door to the Ursuline Convent, both of which are still standing in Quebec City. Some were apparently sheltered with families. As the numbers of recruits grew, Intendant Talon arranged for expanded housing in a private home, owned by Francis Blondeau, across from Quebec City's *Hôtel-Dieu*.

Although actual documentation is lacking, the new arrivals must have been given advice on adapting to married life, keeping a home in a strange and very cold land, and preparing meals with unfamiliar foods. Jeanne, if indeed she was raised in an urban environment as is suspected, would have had to learn about cultivating a garden, raising chickens and pigs, preserving food, preparing meals with unfamiliar ingredients, baking bread, making soap and candles, protecting herself and her family from the cold, illness and insects, and various other tasks.

The new arrivals were kept under close supervision until they married. Visits with suitors occurred on predetermined days of the week in one of three halls. A mystery remains around the criteria for the division, whether according to physical characteristic, social background, place of origin or mere space requirements. Since each man had to apply to the governesses and declare how they made a living and how much property and possessions they owned, it's possible, according to one author, that they were directed to one of the three halls based on the information they provided.

What was it like to be surrounded by men scrutinizing the women to see whether they would make a good wife, mother and helpmate? While the men might have had a dominant role in the mating game, the young women were not passive players. From their conversations on the ship coming from France and then with other women in the colony after they landed, they must have had a good idea of the questions to ask, since they apparently asked a lot of them.

In correspondence to her son, Marie de l'Incarnation, the prominent Ursuline nun who had arrived in Quebec in 1639, listed some of these questions. It would have been amusing to witness the exchanges between the women and their suitors: "What kind of a home do you have? How many rooms are in it? Does it have wooden floors? How many windows? Does the hearth draw well? Have you a proper bed and plenty of blankets?" and "How many acres have you cleared? How many cows, pigs, and sheep do you have? How many chickens?" And then, "How much money have you saved? Are you addicted to drink? Are you of clean habits?"

Love was apparently not very high on the list. Instead, having a home of one's own was one of the most important factors for a *Fille du Roi* in her decision, according to Marie de l'Incarnation. "The smartest [among the suitors] began making some sort of home a year before getting married, because those with a home find a wife more easily. It's the first thing that the girls ask about, wisely at that, since those who are without habitation suffer greatly before becoming comfortable."

The women were generally successful in marrying quickly, with something like 80% of them married within six months. Many who arrived with Jeanne in the summer of 1671 were married much earlier, by October or November and one apparently before the end of August. The choice of husbands was theirs and theirs alone. There was no parental approval required, unlike in France. Some women even changed their minds and had a marriage contract annulled. In the group of women who arrived with Jeanne, 16 of the 120 women, or 13%, sought such annulments. Most of them, however, took only another two to three weeks before marrying someone else.

Prior to the religious ceremony, a couple would have a marriage contract drawn up by a notary—usually ten days prior to the church ceremony. This procedure, unusual in France, was considered necessary in New France because of the lack of family to protect the young women. These documents provide rich information on the couple, such as date and place of baptism, parentage, and sometimes even the occupation of fathers. After their marriage, each couple was said to receive an ox and a cow, two pigs, a pair of chickens, two barrels of salted meat, and some staples, such as wheat, peas and lard—in addition to the young woman's dowry. Such gifts were apparently intended to give the new couples a good start in life together.

Although some of the new couples moved further west along the St. Lawrence to live near Trois-Rivières or Montreal, a large number settled on farms near Quebec City, on Île d'Orleans or in other established settlements on the north shore of the St. Lawrence River. Since these areas closer to Quebec City had already been cleared and developed by earlier colonists, there were often homes, however rustic, on the properties and neighbors to provide support and comfort. And these areas would have been easier to reach. Few roads existed at the time, and many newly-weds would have had to travel in boats or ox-driven carts, or even on foot.

How would these women have been feeling as they left their friends and some semblance of security in Quebec City, Montreal or Trois-Rivières and ventured out into a strange land with a relatively unknown new husband? Were they apprehensive or were they comforted knowing they had a duty to perform for the King—to bear children and make a life for their families in the new world?

***

And fulfill that duty they certainly did. Historian Yves Landry, one of the foremost authorities on these women, in his exhaustive study of the *Filles du Roi* provides many statistics on their lives. Among the women as a whole, the number of marriages for each woman ranged from 0 to 4, and many of these marriages were long ones. Of course, a small number of women went back to France (eight of the 120 in Jeanne's year), some never married (six from Jeanne's group), some were able to obtain a "separation of goods," a form of divorce from their husbands (none in Jeanne's year), and at least one woman became a domestic servant. A few were killed by Iroquois, some died in child birth, or were found frozen in the snow, or died in a shipwreck, or joined the convent. One was even executed for adultery. A few died soon after arriving, and some lived to be well over 90 years old.

The women who remained went on to do their part in colonizing New France. A few women had as many as 18 children, and a small number remained childless. Many had children late into their forties, and many faced early widowhood since the men too often died young from accidents, illness, or war. Widows with small children to raise and no family around needed to marry again quickly. Fortunately, the shortage of women in New France made widows—even those with small children—quite desirable given the number of men who might not have been ready to marry or who might not have found wives in the years of the *Filles du Roi* program. The average time between the death of a spouse and marriage to a new one was 30 months. Some older widows remained that way for the rest of their lives, presumably after being well situated, with their children grown and having a room in their son's or daughter's home.

The goals that Louis the XIV and his minister set for the program were achieved, in the short term at least. In 1663, at the start of the program, the population of New France was less than 3,000. Ten years later it had reached 6,700. And the census taken eight years later, in 1681, counted over 10,000 men, women and children in New France, an estimated three-fold increase over 1663. The program ended in 1673 with the recall of Intendant Talon, the King's administrator for New France, who had been one of the program's champions. It was viewed as sufficiently successful and self-sustaining given the number of births recorded from 1664 on. It's very likely that the war declared on the Dutch by France and England also took the King's attention off the new colony and further burdened France's already strained finances.

***

Trying to understand the reasons why Jeanne and other women chose as they did involves a great deal of speculation because the *Filles du Roi* left no known records or diaries. For many, it was most likely a voluntary decision, although there is evidence of some strong encouragement—even coercion—by guardians, parents, officials at the charity hospitals, parish priests, or recruiters.

While that may have been true for a good number of the women, there were other reasons for leaving France. Certainly they must have heard the rumors and stories from Quebec. Life in the new world would have seemed full of dangers, with its risks from a much harsher climate, unfamiliar environment, and possible attacks by native peoples. Yet, such a possibility could have been seen as a way out, an opportunity to improve their lot in life given their uncertain future in France. Unlike in France, marriage in Canada was a virtual certainty for a woman who wanted to marry despite her age or the size or lack of a dowry. There would certainly be more choices in husbands, in historian Leslie Choquette's words, "from respectable farmers and tradesmen, perhaps even someone of a higher class."

Whatever their reasons or the level of encouragement, the great majority of these women showed incredible courage. They were probably quite out of the ordinary since according to Choquette, migration even within France was rare, especially among single women. Thus these women, Jeanne among them, must have been brave, adventurous women of strong will and stamina, determined to take action and make a good life for themselves and any future families in the new world.

Despite the contribution of these women to the growth of the French colony into the 18th and 19th centuries, confusion has persisted over the years as to whether the *Filles du Roi* were women to marry or "women to enjoy." Erroneous information based on random comments and prejudices on the one side and possible nationalistic pride that has embellished their challenges and legacy on the other have all contributed to the confusion. Historian Landry explained it best by declaring that there is probably an element of truth in both sides of the story. The *Filles du Roi* were not all angels, despite efforts of some French Canadian historians and others to destroy the myth that these founding mothers were prostitutes. There is, indeed, evidence of adultery, even murder, and other crimes, but these incidents represented a very small percentage of the 770 women.

At the same time, they were not fallen women. A review of the data reveal only a rare illegitimate birth either prior to their first marriage in Canada or during their marriages. Many creditable historians find it hard to believe that the King would have provided so much financial support for the emigration of women with sordid pasts and possible disease. After all, his goal was to colonize New France by marrying these women to soldiers, traders, farmers and even men of noble birth. And then there was all that insistence from Minister Colbert and Intendant Talon that the women be healthy and ready for hard farm work!

But legends live on. Is that because the truth is more complicated or less titillating? Or perhaps because such rumors are based on some misogynist perspectives on these independent women who could marry in New France without needing their fathers' or guardians' approval? At a reenactment of the 1664 arrival of the second group of *Filles du Roi* in August, 2014 in Quebec City, a gentleman from Belgium was overheard making a joke about the shady reputation of these women. So even now there appears to be some misunderstanding about them, particularly in Europe where the program is not as well-known as it is in Quebec.

Even with these persistent rumors, there is growing interest in the true lives of these women, the founding mothers of Quebec. *Filles du Roi* societies have sprung up in Quebec and in the United States. With proper documentation, a descendant of one of the *Filles du Roi* is now able to obtain a pin and certificate, attesting to his or her lineage. In the early 1960's, the home where many of the *Filles du Roi* were educated in Montreal became a museum. The last few years have seen more in-depth research on their demographics and contributions. Several romance novels have been published in English and French, based on the lives of different *Filles du Roi*. And in 2013, there were celebrations and a great deal of publicity in Paris, Dieppe, Rouen, La Rochelle, and Quebec to honor the 350th anniversary of the arrival in Quebec of the first group of women.

Part Two

New France 1671–1679

Background on New France and Jeanne's life through the death of her first husband.

3

New France that became Jeanne's Home

In the summer of 1671, after leaving Dieppe sometime in mid to late June and after several weeks at sea, the *Saint Jean-Baptiste* made its way past icebergs, through the dangerous waters of Gaspé Bay, and finally entered the St. Lawrence River. The voyage had apparently been uneventful. Since a marriage contract for one of the *Filles du Roi* on the ship was signed on August 15th, it must have been fairly quick as well.

Nevertheless, Jeanne and the rest of the passengers and crew were probably quite relieved to see land at last. They were perhaps astonished to see the mountain ranges rising up in the distance on both shores. Along the river, dense forests of spruce, fir, oak, birch, and maple trees—of many different shades of green—welcomed them. On the rocky shores or in the occasional meadow, if they sailed close enough to shore, Jeanne might also have caught sight of wolves, moose, bears, beavers, mountain lions, and strange birds watching the ship sail by. Later she would have to get acquainted with the mosquitoes and black flies that would plague the colonists. Until they neared Quebec City, she would not have seen any homes, farms, church steeples, or roads. It was wilderness, a true frontier.

The Quebec that would become Jeanne's home that year was indeed a very different land, she was to learn, from the Normandy that she knew. It had been formed during the Ice Age, as retreating ice cut a narrow valley between two mountain ranges—the Laurentians to the north and the Appalachians to the south—and left behind the 750-mile-long St. Lawrence River, one of the five greatest in the world. In some places it is more than 18 miles across to the other shore. Although difficult to navigate because of its tides and currents, the St. Lawrence would play a major role in the life of the settlement as the major communication and transportation link, in winter as well as summer.

The weather, so different from what Jeanne was used to in Normandy, would also make living in this new land a major challenge. Surely she would have been forewarned that the winter in New France could bring temperatures substantially below freezing and many, many feet of snow. The cold could last for six months. Isolated from the rest of the world, the colony used frozen rivers as major transportation routes. It was often faster, she would discover later, to travel upriver on snowshoes or in a sleigh in winter than by boat during the rest of the year.

In the summer of 1671, the Quebec City that greeted Jeanne and the rest of the ninth contingent of women would have seemed a frontier village compared to thriving towns in France. Today, it is possible to stand in old Quebec City and shut one's eyes and ears to the sounds of cars, buses, and throngs of tourists and find some semblance of 17th century life amid the still-standing buildings and narrow cobblestone streets. When Jeanne arrived, however, Quebec City was a mix of ramshackle buildings and wharves set along the river, with a fortress on the cliff high above, where the Governor's chateau, a church, seminary, convent, and a few other government buildings were located.

Although geographically Quebec City might have reminded Jeanne of Dieppe, it was a much smaller place, with less than 1,000 people living there at the time of her arrival. To be sure, there were more people living in the areas beyond Québec City, but not a great many. By 1671, the colony was expanding out to Île d'Orléans, the large island just east of Quebec City, and along the north shore of the St. Lawrence toward Sainte-Anne-de-Beaupré. The population was moving to the west as well, through Trois-Rivières and to what is now Montreal. The census of 1667 had counted a population of under 4,000 non-native people throughout all of New France. Four years later, after several years of the *Filles du Roi program,* the population had grown, but was still less than 6,000 French inhabitants.

Of course, the French were not the only immigrants to North America at the time. On the Atlantic seaboard, many miles south of Quebec City, the population was growing much more rapidly. A year before Quebec City was founded, English Protestants fleeing from religious persecution in their homeland had established their first settlement in Jamestown, Virginia, on the east coast of what was to become the United States. In 1620 English pilgrims landed on the shores of the Atlantic Ocean north of Jamestown at Plymouth Rock. Five years later, the Dutch established New Amsterdam, at the mouth of the Hudson River, a settlement which later would be named New York. In 1630, Boston, Massachusetts was founded; Harvard College opened its doors six years after that. A printing press was brought to America in 1639; a year later, the first book in America, the *Bay Psalter*, was printed in Boston—all before Jeanne was born.

Unlike New France, where the population was overwhelmingly Catholic and where since the early days of settlement non-Catholics were not allowed to settle permanently or own land, the English and Dutch colonists to the south were decidedly Protestant. Indeed, that part of North America welcomed Huguenots fleeing persecution in France since they, along with other immigrants and natural growth, were helping the European population to rapidly increase.

As time went on, French expansion west and south of New France would threaten another population besides those European neighbors. Expansion would also further endanger already fragile relations with the Amerindians, who despite the cold and other geographic challenges, had inhabited the land for several centuries. The many different tribes of those First Nation peoples had already been decimated by the arrival of the French who brought disease, guns and ambitious plans for the beaver trade and conversion of the native peoples to Christianity. Some tribes appeared to adapt, others moved away, and others continued to be a very real threat to the lives of the French immigrants. For the time being, however, at least when Jeanne arrived in 1671, life in Quebec City and eastwards was relatively safe and calm.

Within New France, efforts had been underway for several years to further settle and organize the colony which was finally beginning to grow. The land around Quebec was being cleared under an arrangement similar to the French feudal system as modified by early French settlers in Quebec. This strategy involved granting large blocks of land, or *seigneuries*, to religious orders or to individuals who would agree to settle the land. At least in the beginning, the recipients of these grants, lords, or s*eigneurs*, were primarily members of the French nobility or soldiers who agreed to remain in New France after their service was ended.

In the early years of the colony, the first grants had been made for land in and around Quebec City, as well as westward toward Trois-Rivières and Montreal. They then began to be extended eastward on Île d'Orléans and along the Beaupré coast, on the north shore of the St. Lawrence around the villages of Château-Richer and L'Ange-Gardien. The land along the southern shore of the St. Lawrence east of Quebec City, however, remained heavily forested. The King had charged his administrator Intendant Jean Talon with ensuring the colony's continued expansion. During the year after Jeanne's arrival, therefore, Talon would begin to make many new land grants along that shore.

In order to create somewhat equal access to the St. Lawrence and a certain amount of consistency in their shape, these seigneuries were usually granted along the river in long narrow rectangles. Within a seigneurial grant, land was arranged in rows, or "*rangs*." The first rang included land directly on the riverbank and was used for the initial grants to settlers. The remaining *rangs* were left for subsequent grants and further development of a seigneurie. Typically, in the first *rang* the seigneur would stake out a personal domain where the family manor would be built. The size of this domain varied from one seigneurie to another. In addition, the seigneur would usually reserve some land not far from the manor for a church and presbytery and for the support of the priest. Many seigneuries also set aside common land for grazing animals. Any oak trees on the land and minerals in the soil remained the property of the King.

As a condition of the grants, seigneurs were required to clear the land and turn forests into farms. To accomplish this goal, seigneurs were expected to bring over settlers, usually with three-year contracts. In exchange for their voyage to New France and the promise of a grant of land at the successful completion of their contracts, these settlers, known as "36-monthers," would clear the seigneur's land and help build his home. At the conclusion of their contracts, the colonists, or *habitants* as they were known then, would receive their own land with the agreement that they would then clear it to further develop the seigneurie.

Within the seigneur's grant, land grants to settlers typically repeated the rectangular pattern of the seigneur's grant. They were long and narrow and usually measured 3 *arpents* wide by 30 *arpents* deep in an attempt to give as many settlers as possible frontage on the river. These patterns, which Jeanne might have seen as the ship neared Quebec City, are still visible on the landscape around Quebec.

Land patterns

The benefits of this pattern were many. It provided equal access to the waterway, usually the St. Lawrence, but other rivers as well. It put homes closer to each other, facilitating travel between neighbors. It also made the land easier to plough, reducing the number of turns necessary once the land was cleared. This arrangement did, however, increase the time a settler might be away from home, clearing or planting the back side of the property.

Besides encouraging settlement of their land, seigneurs were expected to fulfill certain other responsibilities to the King and to their tenants. As soon as a seigneur took possession of his grant, he had to perform an act of homage before the King's representative in the governor's chateau in Quebec City to affirm his commitment to carry out his duties. The seigneur promised to provide an inventory listing tenants and rents due, upon the transfer of the land or upon request from the Intendant. There were also taxes due to the state upon the subsequent sale (but not inheritance) of the seigneurie, in an attempt to discourage trading in land grants.

In addition, seigneurs had responsibilities to their tenants. They were expected to build a manor house where the habitants would pay their taxes. They were expected to provide land for and contribute to the upkeep of a church, construct and maintain a flour mill for settlers, and participate in the building of roads. And since they had the right to administer local justice, they also had to agree to hear cases involving disputes among settlers on their land; most major cases were, however, reserved for the government.

After habitants received their grants of land, they owed the seigneurs taxes that included a small amount of money, several live capons to be brought on St. Martin's Day (November 11) to the seigneur's manor house, and a number of days of annual service, all as specified in their contracts. They committed to fulfill certain other responsibilities, such as building roads, supporting the church, and having their wheat ground at the seigneurial mill when it was built. They were also expected to pay the seigneur a percentage of the sale of land to anyone other than direct family and a designated portion of any fish they caught as well. And they planted the customary Maypole (a fir tree stripped of its branches except at the top) on the seigneur's property every year on May 1—as a tribute to the seigneur.

Relations between the habitants and seigneurs were generally said to be closer and friendlier than in France at the time since both were working against an unsettled wilderness. Jeanne's life would appear to subsequently prove this to be true. The houses of the seigneurs were usually larger, sometimes made of stone, and more comfortable than those of the habitants, but they were not the castles still visible in France. Habitants eventually had land of their own, had more freedom and plenty of firewood, and could hunt and fish legally, unlike their counterparts in France where normally only nobles had these privileges.

They also paid fewer taxes than in France since there was no *taille*, or head tax, no salt tax, or other punishing financial obligations. Finally, in the 17th century and into the early 18th, their land was not devastated by war.

Seigneurial pew

For seigneurs, it was a different story. It's true they were granted a pew in a position of honor in the church, usually facing the pulpit, and they had the right to be buried under the seigneurial pew. They could carry a sword and had a title of "knight" or *ecuyer*. And seigneuries, along with church parishes, served as units of local government, defense, and community life.

Even with these privileges, they were apparently less well off than their peers in France, at least financially. According to research conducted by Richard Colebrook Harris in his book *The Seigneurial System in Early Canada*, most seigneuries were rarely very profitable, despite the income from taxes and other revenues and despite the absence of financial obligations faced by their French counterparts. The system seems to have been created and maintained as a means toward colonization and settlement, as opposed to a path to wealth and power for seigneurs.

This arrangement of land settlement by seigneurs and habitants was not played out uniformly across 17th century Quebec. Some seigneurs did apparently take their responsibilities and their promise to the King seriously. They brought in new settlers, worked with their habitants to clear and develop the land, made subsequent grants to those men with whom they had contracts, and maintained residences on their seigneuries. Others, apparently the majority in fact, remained in Quebec City or Montreal, preferring to enjoy a more "courtly" life there. They failed to develop their grants, despite threats from the King that their seigneuries might be confiscated if they were not developed.

Similarly, not all colonists chose to settle down to clear and then eventually develop their own land. Clearing land and farming it were tough, difficult tasks that took many months or even several years to complete. Habitants often needed to continue working a trade to bring in income to fund purchases of materials and tools for their farms. Some newcomers chose alternative life styles, taking up trapping and the fur trade, for example, a life of great freedom but not without several lethal threats from the demands of the work, frigid winters, wild animals, and the discontented native population. Other colonists chose to rent already cleared land to get a jump start on settlement. Others elected to trade in grants, buying and selling land and leasing it out again. And still others chose to stay in Quebec City or Montreal and set up shop as merchants or artisans.

To fulfill his dreams and grow the colony, the King knew he needed not only the labor and output of all these men in their various occupations. He also needed them to remain in the colony and start families. The *Filles du Roi* program was only one of the initiatives he and his ministers were taking to grow the colony and make it self-sufficient, but it certainly was an early success.

How must Jeanne have felt when she and the other *Filles du Roi* saw those throngs of men and the cheering crowds shouting welcome at the ship's arrival? Once they had disembarked, it probably took some time for them to lose their sea legs and walk steadily on land where they were met by the King's representatives and escorted to their new, though temporary, homes in New France. On the way, did Jeanne think to herself, "What have I done?" or was she both excited and scared about the adventure ahead? And was she wondering, "How shall I choose a husband from all these men?" and "How much time can I take to decide?"

4

Jeanne's First Husband

Within two months of her arrival, Jeanne married Guillaume Lecanteur on Monday, October 19, 1671 in Notre-Dame church in Quebec City's upper town. Theirs was among the earliest marriages for the group that arrived that year.

Who was this man, Jeanne's first husband? Little is actually known about him, perhaps because he left no descendants. Their marriage contract, signed eight days before their marriage, described his parents as the deceased Nicolas Lecanteur and Jeanne Hamelot, from St. Sauveur parish, in Beaumont-en-Auge, France, a small hilltop village not far from Pont-L'Evêque and Honfleur, in the middle of Normandy.

Beaumont-en-Auge

According to the *Fichier Origine*, a database developed and maintained by two federations of genealogical societies in Quebec, his birthdate is given as "about 1646," although his actual baptismal record has not been found. An on-site search of the parish records at the archives in Caen confirmed the absence of a record for Lecanteur. It is possible that his baptism was not registered; however, another possibility exists. When a date of birth was not listed on a marriage contract and no later information, such as census data, was to be found, researchers often just subtracted the age of majority (25 at the time) from the date of marriage to come up with an approximate birthdate, such as "about 1646." However, the registers for the parish in Beaumont-en-Auge prior to January 1, 1645 are missing, and records for his sisters have in fact been located in the archives after that date. Thus, it is more than likely that he was born before January 1,1645 and that his baptismal act is among those missing registers.

The *Fichier* database researchers have found a little information about his family. Lecanteur apparently had two sisters, a sister Marie born on March 21, 1645, and one named Guillemette who married in 1666, four years after their father died. That is all that is known about his family in France. Did he leave his mother and sisters behind to seek his fortune in New France?

In the records located to date in Quebec, Lecanteur is frequently referred to "dit la Tour" and as "Sieur de La Tour." "Dit" names were often used as nicknames especially with soldiers, describing personal characteristics or place of origin. It is not inconceivable that the "la Tour" nickname referred to Lecanteur's height, since "tour" translates into English as "tower." The title "Sieur de la Tour" provides another piece of information about Jeanne's first husband. Roughly translated as "Mister from la Tour," the term usually implied some level of respect, even a higher rank in society, perhaps a member of the "petite bourgeoisie." His signature would bolster that conjecture, since he signed his name with quite a flamboyant flourish, revealing a good deal of education. Archivists in Caen, where the parish records for Beaumont-en-Auge are located, suggested that his signature indicated he was probably a merchant or lawyer and would have been educated in Caen or Le Havre, or possibly Rouen.

Signature of Guillaume Lecanteur

Notarial records in Quebec confirm that the man who was to become Jeanne's first husband was already in Quebec in 1670, at least a year before Jeanne arrived. Because he was not listed in either the 1666 or 1667 census, it is most likely that he arrived after that date—although the census count was not always 100% accurate. Information about how or when he arrived in Quebec is missing. He is not listed as a soldier in the Carignan regiments or any later regiments and never identified himself as a "soldier." There are no ship records that list his passage and no documents that describe any association he might have had with others in Quebec even though independent travelers who paid their own way were rare at the time. It is possible, given assumptions about his education, that he joined up with a group of merchants, to seek his fortune in New France. The 1670 grant was made by Toussaint Toupin, a prominent businessman in Quebec, who could have recruited Lecanteur to the colony, thus providing another explanation.

The questions continue. The marriage contract with Jeanne lists Lecanteur as a "*habitant*," or farmer, and as being from Boyer Point, La Durantaye. There are no records that Lecanteur had land or resided there. Given that at the time of their marriage he had actually leased land elsewhere, it is puzzling why the marriage contract contained this reference. There are of course some possible explanations. One is that Lecanteur had met Olivier Morel de la Durantaye, the eventual seigneur of the grant that bore his name, upon his arrival in Quebec and had some verbal agreement about a grant on Morel de la Durantaye's land. Or perhaps one of the young men in the circle of friends that Lecanteur apparently was developing knew Morel de la Durantaye and introduced the two men who then proceeded to work out a deal?

Another possible explanation, perhaps even more creditable, exists. One of the other grooms being married the same day as Jeanne and Lecanteur was in fact working for Morel de la Durantaye. Lecanteur could have used that reference since he lacked a permanent residence at the time, or the clerk could have made a mistake and misunderstood Lecanteur.

His land dealings added to the mystery that surrounded Lecanteur. On July 9, 1670, Lecanteur had received that small grant for land along the Charles River from Toussaint Toupin. Assuming the records are correct, the grant would have been at the base of Avenue Saint Sacrement, in the St. Foy district of Quebec City. It is now a peaceful cemetery, set beside the river. As a grant, back in 1670, it still needed to be cleared and, though not large in comparison to other grants at the time, it still would have required a lot of hard work and many months to turn it into a farm. Similar to so many other immigrants, Lecanteur probably had little to no farming experience. Apparently, he did not do much to develop the property since when he sold it a year later, it is not certain how much, if any, of it was cleared.

In October 1670, three months after receiving that grant and a year before he married Jeanne, Lecanteur signed an agreement with one Claude Gratton to help him clear his land. The outcome of this agreement is unknown, but Lecanteur appears to have broken it in search of something more to his liking. Within six days, he signed a lease with Toupin for a larger grant of uncleared land further east of Quebec City on the north shore of the St. Lawrence River. He apparently changed his mind and annulled the lease after less than a month. In September of the following year, Lecanteur sold the land he had been granted along the Charles River. By the time he executed that sale, he must have already met Jeanne since they were married a month later.

When Lecanteur did meet Jeanne, it is not clear where he was actually living. But he apparently had found a place for his new family. A day before they were married on October 19, 1671, he signed a two-year lease for what appears to have been a farm in la Petite-Auvergne, near Charlesbourg, one of the first planned villages in New France, not far from Quebec City.

Why Jeanne was attracted to this enigmatic man and why she decided to marry him after such a short courtship are more matters of speculation. No one was forcing her to choose, and she needed no one's approval, as would have been the case in France. Of course, as a *Fille du Roi* she was under some pressure to marry soon after reaching New France. The young women were given housing for a short period of time until they could marry and start to fulfil the purpose for their journey. At the same time, Jeanne was one of approximately twenty women in Quebec City who married within less than three months of their arrival, when the average interval was closer to six months. She clearly made her decision more quickly than most of the other women in her contingent.

Since the new arrivals were said to have peppered potential mates with questions about their suitability, did Jeanne ask all those questions about his home, his farm, and his habits when they met? What did he tell her about the home he had found for them? Was she at all concerned about any discrepancies between the marriage contract and his answers?

The lease on the land in la Petite-Auvergne must have provided satisfactory answers to any questions she might have had. Perhaps the promise of a home, no matter how lowly, not far from Quebec City might have seemed safe. Unlike many of the other *Filles du Roi*, they would not be moving out into the wilderness, where they could face dangers from wild animals and Amerindians. Instead they would be staying closer to Quebec City on land that was already somewhat developed and held the promise of neighbors. In fact, she might have known other *Filles du Roi* who had arrived with her the previous summer and who were also moving to the area.

The reasons for Jeanne's personal attraction to Lecanteur are speculative at best. It could have been because they shared a common dialect, both coming from Normandy. Or perhaps she was just eager to get her life settled. Another possible reason was that he did not seem to be a typical habitant. Did the suggestion of a higher class from his name attract her? Perhaps he had a dashing demeanor and figure, possibly tall, to match the flourish in his signature? If indeed she had noble origins, even from the lesser nobility, his manners could have appeared more familiar and attractive to her. Or perhaps he was just more refined, had more friends, or could even have smelled better than the other men.

Her possible upbringing could also explain Lecanteur's interest in

Jeanne. If it is assumed that he had a middle class upbringing and was educated, then something special about Jeanne must have attracted him. Perhaps she had more charm and urban sophistication than many of the other women. Or she was prettier or appeared stronger and more intelligent. Or, perhaps she was indeed from a better family as that historian from Rouen believes and that sort of upbringing was important to him.

Whatever the reasons behind their choice, they entered into a marriage contract on the morning of October 11, 1671, in the home of Anne Gasnier, one of the governesses of the *Filles du Roi* contingents. The contract provides a great deal of information on Jeanne, some of it adding to the confusion. It states that she was the daughter of Jacques Alexander and Marguerite Scomant, from the parish of St. Jacques in Dieppe. Since the contract was the first instance that Jeanne's mother's name appeared in writing, this could have been the occasion for the misinterpretation of the spelling of "Escoulant," which would eventually be carried over into Jeanne's next contracts.

This was also the point where some historians have taken Jeanne's place of birth or baptism to be Dieppe even though the contract only stated that her parents were from Dieppe, not that she was born there. According to respected historians, place of origin did not necessarily mean place of birth or baptism. Instead, it could have referred to the last residence of an immigrant or of his or her parents or the parish where he/she was best known.

The contract then went on to describe Jeanne's possessions, her "trousseau," as being valued at 300 livres, and then specifically mentioned her dowry of 50 livres "which his Majesty has given her in consideration of her marriage." She kept half of her trousseau as her personal property and gave the other half to their community property. Lecanteur, in exchange, promised a comparable contribution to their marriage of 300 livres.

They both promised to take each other as husband and wife and to hold the rest of their possessions as community property. Any debts that either Jeanne or Lecanteur had incurred prior to their marriage were not recognized as belonging to the community and were to be paid by the individual responsible for them. The contract was then signed by several witnesses, possibly friends of Lecanteur, some of them men with rather elaborate signatures, similar to Lecanteur's.

Eight days later, on October 19, they were married in Notre-Dame church, in upper Quebec City, along with nine other couples. Their marriage record confirmed that banns of marriage had been published twice, with the third bann usually required by the church having been dispensed with by the Bishop. On the record, Lecanteur's father is listed as deceased as is Jeanne's father. Jeanne's mother's name was now written as "Scorban."

What must the ceremony have been like? Were there separate ceremonies or just one large one with a communal blessing by the priest for all those marrying that day? Most certainly, long trailing white dresses, veils and organ music were missing. Were there flowers or just solemn oaths, "until death do us part" and then individual registrations of their marriage in the parish book?

Notre-Dame Cathedral in Quebec

5

Life on the north shore of the St. Lawrence River 1671–1679

If Jeanne and Lecanteur were typical of many other *Filles du Roi* couples, upon their marriage they would have collected Jeanne's promised dowry of 50 livres, along with the King's gifts of farm animals, barrels of salted meat, and other staples. They then had to transport themselves and their provisions in a cart pulled by dogs or an ox, to the farm in la Petite-Auvergne that Guilllaume had leased from Adrien Michelon the day before their wedding. While la Petite-Auvergne is less than seven kilometers northwest of Quebec City, there were no direct roads to their place at the time. They would first have had to be ferried across the Charles River. Then they would have had to travel the dirt, possibly muddy, paths that existed at the time. They would have had to walk around the bog at the base of the hill and up and across in a circuitous route to their new home.

The farm, according to the maps at *La Société d'Histoire de Charlesbourg*, would have had a lovely view of Quebec City, set as it was on a hill above that bog. The view might have generated a spirit of hope in Jeanne for her life ahead. In spite of its possible setting, Jeanne might have been a bit disappointed when she first saw the home her new husband had readied for them, given what she might have known in France. Or perhaps, she was just happy to be settled so that the tiny, rustic wooden cabin with its dirt floor, simple stove, and thatched roof did not bother her. The one room would be both their kitchen and their bedroom. Oiled skins served as windows. If they were lucky, there was also a small building to be used as a barn and stable.

In all likelihood, their home was primitive and spartan, with little furniture, other than a bed, a table, a couple of chairs, the trunk that Jeanne had brought with her from France, and perhaps a cupboard. She probably had brought some linen for the bed with her as part of her "trousseau." She would not have to worry about changing clothes. She would learn, if she had not already, that people in New France were like their families in France. They generally washed their face and hands in cold water each morning, but all-over bathing and changing clothes were done only rarely, and only when entirely necessary.

Their home would have been surrounded by wheat farms. Although nearly 60 families were living in the area on those farms and some of those families were couples married on the same day as Jeanne and Lecanteur, Jeanne would not have had much time to visit with old friends or make new ones. They only had a few weeks after their arrival to get ready for her first Canadian winter. She probably was not able to even take a moment to look around and wonder at the changing colors on the landscape of her new homeland.

Jeanne and her new husband first needed to settle in with the provisions they had brought with them or that Lecanteur had arranged for in advance. They then would have had to check to see what they could harvest from any existing garden or what they would have to borrow from neighbors to prepare for the winter ahead. Jeanne would have had to start applying the lessons she had learned in Quebec City about cooking with strange fruits and vegetables, such as pumpkins, melons, squash, gooseberries and cranberries, and all kinds of wild game. She had to figure out how to sweeten their food with maple sugar, how to bake several loaves of bread, instead of buying it in a local market, to season their meals with herbs that were unavailable in France, and to use native plants to make natural medicines and remedies. Any recipes she would have brought with her from France would have had to have been by memory and would have had to be adapted in her new home.

With winter coming, they would have had to repair the cabin and get it ready for the cold and wind and cut enough wood to keep them warm. A supply of candles for the long winter nights would have had to be secured. They would also have had to store vegetables, dry meat, and care for the animals they had brought with them. They may or may not have had a root cellar for storing their food for winter. Lecanteur may have had some farm work to finish up before the snows came and arrangements to be made to have whatever wheat he could harvest from the fields ground at the local mill.

Jeanne probably did not have much more than rudimentary utensils to work with, one or two pots and a few spoons, forks, knives, plates and bowls. To keep the dust down on their dirt floor, she would just sprinkle some water around. Apparently, there was little obsession with cleanliness at the time and no awareness of the connection between germs and disease.

Her clothes from France had to serve for many years. Any rips or tears would have to be mended, as best she could. She would have to get used to wearing skirts that were much shorter than in France and to putting on clogs made of cowhide, both of which were required for the work in the garden and the fields.

When winter and snow arrived within a few weeks after their arrival, the cold would not have been like anything Jeanne would have known before. Even though she might have thought it beautiful at first, it could only have added to a sense of isolation. Often in the winter they might only hear the sound of wind, which could be fierce at times, and falling snow. While they might have been able to light up their home with candles at night, the darkness could have reminded Jeanne of the nights on the ship when they had only moon and stars to light their way.

In the middle of this new world with its different climate and approaching winter, she also had to adapt to living with a man. This would be the first chapter in their life together. Did she have time during that first winter to make friends with neighbors who could help her adjust to this new life? Did she ever try to stay in touch with other women who had come with her on the ship and lived nearby?

In the spring, assuming they stayed that long, Jeanne would have done her best to get any existing garden replanted. Lecanteur would have been obligated to continue to clear the land, plant it with the seeds they had been given upon their marriage, and pay Michelon the agreed-to share of produce. Soon, however, they were making plans to move.

By the fall of 1672, they were living in L'Ange-Gardien. No information has been found to explain why they abandoned their lease on the farm in la Petite-Auvergne. Perhaps it was too far from the St. Lawrence River, or the farm's location and the terms of the lease were not to Lecanteur's liking. Whatever the reasons, they would have had to travel back to Quebec City, with their household goods and any animals. They then would have had to either take a boat or walk along the path that would one day become the *Chemin du Roi* to reach their new home some 25 kilometers northeast of Quebec City, along the northern shore of the St. Lawrence River.

When they made this trip, Jeanne was pregnant with their first child. She would have learned to use some of those 1,000 pins she had been given when she left France to loosen her bodice and skirt as her pregnancy progressed. Their first son Nicolas was baptized in the church at Château-Richer, the village next to L'Ange-Gardien, on September 7, 1672. It does not appear that they actually had a home in Château-Richer. It's more likely that the baptism was recorded as having taken place in that village because of the availability of a priest.

Their actual home was in fact in L'Ange-Gardien. Although the notarial record of a lease of the property in that location is missing, Lecanteur's subsequent purchase of the property two years later includes a reference to a 1672 lease. The property included a home of some sort, a barn, and a stable. As part of the subsequent purchase, it came with a pair of oxen and a plow. It was located next door to the LeTarte family who would eventually play a major role in Jeanne's life.

During the time that Jeanne was busy with getting settled, caring for their new son, keeping house, and reconnecting with friends and other *Filles du Roi* living nearby, Lecanteur apparently was in the process of making connections and seeking new land deals. On November

11, 1672, two months after Nicolas was born, Lecanteur purchased partially cleared land with a small cabin in Berthier sur Mer, on the south shore of the St. Lawrence, on the other side of Île d'Orléans.

There is no evidence that they moved across the river. Instead, Jeanne and Lecanteur were building a community in L'Ange-Gardien. Jeanne could finally set up home, learn more about adapting to life in New France from neighbors, many of whom were from Normandy like Jeanne and Lecanteur and many of whom would serve as godparents to their children. Registers recorded their attendance at a baptism and a wedding in L'Ange-Gardien. And in November, 1674, Lecanteur bought the land he had been leasing in L'Ange-Gardien for 1,500 livres. Their second son Charles was baptized there a year later in December.

In 1676 Lecanteur was a defendant in a civil case. Since the land in Berthier appears to have been returned to its owner, he seems to have defaulted on paying the taxes required at the time of the purchase of land in L'Ange-Gardien. The facts about the case are somewhat unclear, but he definitely lost. He claimed he could not pay the fine levied on him because he no longer had the land in question and had no means of paying the fine. If he indeed no longer had the property, it is unclear where they were then making their home.

Interestingly, the judgment against him did not appear to keep him from buying more land. On June 22, 1677, Lecanteur bought partially cleared land with a small cabin in the parish of St. Pierre, on Île d'Orléans across the St. Lawrence River from L'Ange-Gardien. Perhaps they were making plans to move. This time both his and Jeanne's names appeared on the contract. How he got the money is unknown. Evidently there were people ready to lend money in exchange for agreements to work the land. According to Louise Dechêne, in her landmark book on habitants and merchants in Montreal, buyers who were eager to deal in land holdings but who had no savings could provide a small down payment, with the remainder to be paid in produce over several years—at least up until 1680 when credit tightened up.

Within twelve months, however, that sale was annulled. Then, just a month after the disposition of the land, their third son was born and baptized on July 24, 1678 in L'Ange-Gardien. According to one record, Lecanteur was listed as "present." But the records are quite confusing. In one register the baby was listed as "unnamed," yet in another he was identified as "Guillaume." And his father's presence is not officially acknowledged. Later events confirm that he was, in all likelihood, not in attendance.

In any case, Jeanne was still apparently living in L'Ange-Gardien, possibly with friends. She was on her own, however, because around the time of her third son's birth, her husband disappeared. By the end of 1678, Jeanne was alone, left with a newborn son, two other sons under the age of seven, and debts. No death certificate has been found for her husband, despite attempts to locate it. Since the evidence is mixed on whether he attended his son's baptism in July, the date and circumstances of his death are a mystery. When? Where? And how did he die? Had he perhaps hired himself out as an explorer or fur trader in those last years to earn money to pay off his debts or to escape from them and then suffered a fatal accident? Later documents indicated that there must have been witnesses to his death and that he was probably buried where he died, too far from a church for his death to be recorded. It's also possible that any existing records were lost since the death records for L'Ange-Gardien for those years are missing in the microfilm files.

***

In the archives in Montreal, a book about the Lévesque family briefly refers to Lecanteur as possessing "la bougeotte." That's the French term for having "itchy feet." This reference to a lack of ability to commit seems to fit his life. The question though really is, was this unusual behavior for a man of that time? Was Lecanteur "poor and unstable," as another author wrote, or was he just one of a group of entrepreneurial men, typical of early Canada?

In actuality, it seems that the latter is more likely, at least according to historian Silvio Dumas with concurrence from one of the respected archivists in Quebec City. Dumas wrote in his book on the *Filles du Roi* (roughly translated):

> Several men who married the *Filles du Roi* had 'the mania of the *bourgeotte.*' It was not rare to find these pioneers who marry in Quebec City, have their first child there, a second in Trois-Rivières, and a third in Montreal.

No matter whether Guillllaume Lecanteur was typical of other men at the time or not, he was her husband. How did Jeanne feel when she heard the news? Despair for the future, especially looking over what she had left and having no home but relying on the charity of friends? Grief at the loss of her husband? Shame from the debts he left behind? Perhaps even some relief? Life with Lecanteur could not have been easy. Instead of an entrepreneurial land trader, he might indeed have been unstable, a scoundrel, or a man avoiding commitment, easily bored, and with "itchy feet." Whatever the real story, it could not have been a comfortable life.

But what could she have done if she had wanted a change? Lecanteur would have made all the decisions, a privilege held by men at that time, similar to their situation in France. Single and married women had few, if any, rights of their own, so it's not known if Jeanne played a role in any major decisions. She had married her husband in the Catholic Church—for life… "until death us do part." While some women did arrange for a "separation of goods," Jeanne had three children and she would have had to take care of them on her own. There is no evidence she had any craft or skill to try to survive as a single mother. Had she ever taken time to reflect on any options, or did she just live day to day with the more mundane, but very demanding tasks of keeping a home and raising young children? Perhaps at the time, her worldview was too limited and she could not have imagined any other life? Was she possibly ruing her decision to come to New France?

It must have been a frightening situation when she found out he was gone. Although she surely had the support of friends in the community, her options were few. Even though she somehow had managed to hold on to her dowry, she had few other resources. It might have been possible for some women at the time to start a business or enter the convent, at least according to Canadian historian Jan Noel in her book *Along the River.* Both options, however, required more resources than Jeanne had at the time. She could not go back to France—again such a voyage required money and she did not have family or any good prospects back in France, at least as far as is known. Even if there were family, they probably could not have offered help. It might have been just her mother, but by 1678 even she might have died or been sick, or, if alive, incapable of caring for Jeanne and her family. Would any relatives, even if they had some resources as members of the lower nobility, have wanted her back—especially now with three young children and given the economic situation in France?

Because of the lack of women in the colony at the time, widows with an inheritance or with property remarried quickly. A house, tools, land already cleared made them attractive partners to bachelors. But Jeanne had nothing. Lecanteur had left her with no means of supporting their family. A widow with small children could hardly farm the land alone.

Jeanne faced widowhood, poverty, and was alone and unprotected in a wild, still untamed country. She did not have family to turn to for advice and would have had to rely on friends and neighbors, but it was a decision that was hers alone to make. Her only hope, her only option, for herself and her family, was to marry again.

Part Three

Rivierè-Ouelle 1679-1699

Jeanne's life in Rivière-Ouelle, her new home

6

Jean-Baptiste-François Deschamps de la Bouteillerie

During those eight years from 1671 to 1679 while Jeanne was dealing with the changes and challenges of life with Lecanteur, there were also changes elsewhere in New France. The year after Jeanne moved from la Petite-Auvergne to L'Ange-Gardien and delivered her first child, geographer Louis Joliet and Jesuit Father Jacques Marquette reached the upper Mississippi River. New France would soon extend up to Hudson Bay out past the Great Lakes and down to present day Louisiana. The Atlantic seaboard remained in the hands of the English and the Dutch.

Within what is now Quebec, colonists were continuing to develop land along the north shore of the St. Lawrence, around Montreal, Trois-Rivières, and Quebec City and to the east on Île d'Orléans and out to Sainte-Anne-de-Beaupré. The south shore of the St. Lawrence River, both west and east of Quebec City, still needed colonists. To address this void and continue the colony's expansion, in 1672 Intendant Jean Talon, the King's administrative chief in New France, had given out 55 grants of land, most of them located on the south shore of the St. Lawrence River. One of those seigneuries was granted to Jean-Baptiste-François Deschamps de la Bouteillerie in October of that year.

Deschamps had arrived in New France from Dieppe in the summer of 1671. In fact his departure is noted in a passage from the book *Antiquitez et Chroniques de la Ville de Dieppe ("Annals and Chronicles of the City of Dieppe")*. The original book was written in 1682, just eleven years after the ship's departure, by David Asseline, a priest turned historian, who lived in Dieppe and who was known for his meticulous research.

According to Asseline, in late June, 1671, the 300-ton ship "*Le Saint Jean-Baptiste*" left Dieppe harbor headed for Quebec. On board was a young "gentleman," "le sieur de la Bouteillerie," from the Pays de Caux. He brought with him two carpenters, two masons, and four laborers to settle the land which the King had given him. This land, approximately 1,000 arpents, or about 1.32 square miles, was reported to be located between the towns of Trois-Rivières and Montreal. Also on board were one hundred men, 120 young women from Paris[1], ten mules, 50 male sheep, dry goods, blankets, and many other items and animals that would be useful to those living in New France or for the voyage. Six months later, the ship brought back to Dieppe 10,000 pounds of beaver skins, 400 moose skins, a supply of pitch, and many rarities, among them a live, approximately six-month-old moose, a fox, and a dozen large birds to be given to the King.

Cliponville church

The young gentleman, Jean-Baptiste-François Deschamps de la Bouteillerie, was born sometime around 1646 in Cliponville, a small Norman village just to the northwest of Yvetot and not far from Rouen. While his baptismal record has not been found and there is thus no accurate date of birth, later records give an approximate year for his birth. However, marriage documents do provide the names of his parents. He was one of at least 11 children born to Jean Deschamps de Boishébert and Elizabeth, or Isabeau, de Bin.

1 In the original version of his book, Asseline used a strange number when counting the young women on board. It has sometimes been translated as "26," but that appears to be a mistake. According to a later interpretation written 100 years later and with the concurrence of an archivist in Dieppe who reviewed the original, the number was most likely six times 20, or 120. However, this number can also be questioned for two reasons. It would represent the total contingent of *Filles du Roi* for the year 1671 and there is some conjecture that there were other ships delivering these young women to New France that year. In addition, not all the young women were from Paris.

Jean-Baptiste's family, by some reports, could trace its line back at least to the third crusade. While this long lineage has been questioned as more legend than fact, his family could trace its noble roots back for at least several centuries. The various books on the nobility in Normandy provide a genealogy that traces Jean-Baptiste's male line starting with Robin, or Robert Deschamps, who was ennobled on July 28, 1437 by French King Charles VII in return for his support during the war with England. Robert's father had been mayor of Rouen in 1382. His uncle, Gilles, had served as the King's ambassador to the pope and was named bishop of Coutances in 1411. Gilles was buried in the Cathedral in Rouen in 1413.

The Deschamps line then endured down through the centuries. Through acquisitions of "fiefs" or "seigneuries" by means of purchases, marriage alliances, and further recognition of service to French kings, their property continued to grow in the Pays de Caux north of Rouen. Jean-Baptiste's grandfather Charles obtained the Boishébert fief and thus the title "de Boishébert." Along the way, the family acquired a coat of arms: three green parrots against a silver background.

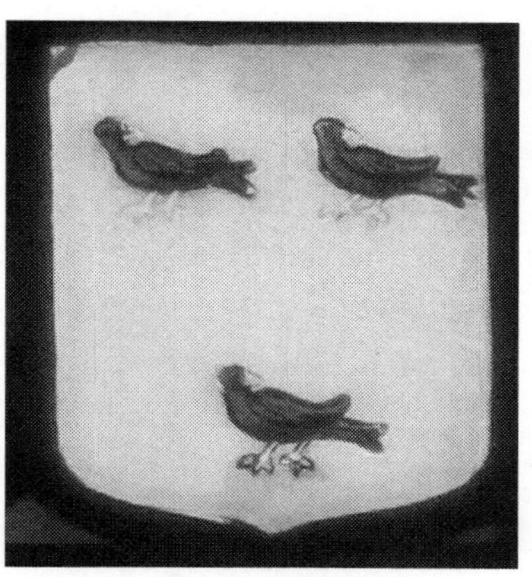

de Boishébert coat of arms from the church in Envronville

Charles married Suzanne Le Bouteiller, who brought into the family the fief of La Bouteillerie that she had inherited from her father, thus extending the boundaries of the family's holdings. One of the daughters of that marriage, Marie Deschamps, had entered the Augustinian monastery of the Hospitalières in Dieppe under the name Saint Joachim. In 1643, she was one of that small group of nuns who journeyed to New France to support the work of the recently founded *Hôtel-Dieu*, in Quebec City.

Jean-Baptiste's father, Jean Deschamps de Boishébert, was Seigneur de Costecoste, de Montaubert, and des Landes and had been honored by Louis XIII in 1629 for the service that he and his family had rendered to the kings of France. He was also a surgeon and along with his brother, who was also a surgeon, happened to provide many months of care to the father of the philosopher Blaise Pascal after an accident in Rouen. During these months, they are reported to have converted to the principles of Jansenism, a "conservative branch" of the Catholic Church that had sprung up in response to the growing threat of Protestantism and to the need to reform the ways of errant priests.

The economic situation of the family in the first half of the 17th century is unknown. They apparently had a manor home in Cliponville and owned several fiefs or seigneuries, around the villages of Cliponville, Envronville, and Hautot-le-Vatois, not far from Dieppe or Rouen. The family archives unfortunately were destroyed during World War II in the fighting near Dieppe. Thus, their role in the *Fronde*, any judicial or administrative responsibilities they might have held, or their financial stability all remain lost to history. Were their positions in society, as members of the more ancient noble class, threatened by the sale of offices and titles by the King and his administrators? Were their fortunes declining as the number of branches of the family requiring financial resources grew at the same time that revenues were falling as a result of worsening economic conditions that challenged their tenants' ability to pay their rents? Or were they able to remain relatively prosperous as their family's subsequent history might suggest?

What is known about the family is that in keeping with the practice and laws of the times, Adrien, the third Deschamps son and the older brother of Jean-Baptiste, inherited the family's title and their fairly large land holdings since the first son died without having married and the second became a priest. The remaining seven children apparently either joined the priesthood or the convent or died without progeny. Adrien went on to have a long lineage in France, including many descendants who still live in that part of France. He died on December 17, 1703 in Cliponville, leaving two sons.

Signature of Deschamps

Jean-Baptiste's signature on later documents indicates he was well-educated, but the kind of education he received has not been recorded. Growing up as a young nobleman in Normandy, he would first have been tutored at home by his mother or grandmother and then later received an education in law, philosophy, Latin, religion, the arts and science in a private military school, as an uncle had, or in a seminary. Such an education would have prepared him to take up a career in the military, at court, as a lawyer, or with the church, or even possibly to follow in his father's footsteps as a doctor. He must also have learned some of the fundamentals of managing an estate from his father.

Although not the primary inheritor of his family's estate, Jean-Baptiste did inherit the title *La Bouteillerie* that had been passed down from his grandmother who died in 1654 when Jean-Baptiste would have been around 8 years old. It's not known if along with the title came any revenues from the estate.

With little chance of much inheritance other than that title and with a future in the military or with the church, either of which he could have found limiting, dismal, or frustrating, he instead decided on another path: adventure. He chose to explore possibilities in New France, an opportunity which apparently far outweighed any fears of a dangerous crossing or the prospects of a harsh life there. Perhaps he had even received letters from his aunt, the Augustinian nun Sister St. Joachim who had preceded him to Quebec decades earlier, encouraging him to try his luck in New France.

As the story goes, in return for the promise of a substantial land grant from the King, Deschamps agreed to use the grant to help colonize New France and to invest his own money to develop it. Somehow Deschamps was able to persuade those eight men to join him on the ship that left Dieppe in late June, 1671.

It's possible—even fun—to speculate on the number of conversations required to convince Robert Lévesque, Damien Bérubé, Jacques Thiboutout, and other countrymen from nearby villages to join him on this adventure in New France. How persuasive did he need to be? Did they see his proposal as an opportunity or too risky a venture?

He was offering them a three-year contract to help him clear the land and build him a home on his land. In exchange, he would provide their passage to New France, room and board for those three years, and then land grants of their own upon completion of their contracts.

Eight accepted but how many others declined? How did he manage to gather together the men who accepted his offer to discuss their concerns, worries, and questions, without telephones or the Internet? How did they go about gathering information about what to expect, given limited contact with those in New France? Perhaps they asked around for stories in the marketplace in nearby Yvetot, Rouen or Dieppe, since by 1671 there should have been several decades of lessons from explorers and others who had ventured to New France.

And it might be easy to imagine the conversations among those who finally gathered to plan for the trip: "What should we bring? What kind of tools do we need? How many? Can we find them in Quebec or do we need to bring them with us?" And then, even more profoundly, "How can we guard against seasickness and other diseases?" "How much food and drink do we need to bring for the trip?" and "How do we protect ourselves in storms or in an attack by pirates?"

After what was at least a six-week journey, they landed in New France. While there is no documentation to define exactly what the men did after their arrival, they probably went right to work. Presumably, their three-year contracts started when they boarded the ship in France, and those contracts of engagement prohibited them from doing any other work or marrying until completion. It is hard to believe that Deschamps would let them sit idle for a year until his grant was official. And in fact the grant, when it was issued in October 1672, did state that Deschamps had already started work on the land.

Thus, they must have done some reconnaissance prior to arriving in Quebec, had some planning sessions on the ship on the way over, in between bouts of seasickness, or quickly began to scout out possible locations for Deschamps' grant as soon as they landed in Quebec. After all, they only had a short time to find the land to be granted and start to work before the snows started.

The most likely scenario is that Deschamps had obtained some sort of promise of a grant prior to or just after arrival. They then gathered the necessary tools and supplies, arranged for transport of themselves and any animals, and all headed over to that site. There they would have camped out, throwing up some rudimentary dwellings to protect themselves and their animals from the winter snows. Deschamps would have had to figure out where to locate his manor home. Then he and the men spent the next three years clearing land and building a home for Deschamps and cabins for themselves.

Despite Asseline's reference to a promised land grant between Trois-Rivières and Montreal, of which there is no record, the land Deschamps was officially granted by Intendant Talon on October 29, 1672 lay in the opposite direction, 148 kilometers northeast of Quebec City. One of the most easterly seigneuries at the time to be granted on the south shore of the St. Lawrence River, it was apparently named "Rivière-Ouelle" in honor of Louis Houel, a companion of explorer Samuel Champlain and possibly a friend of the Deschamps family. It was also known as "La Bouteillerie," in honor of Deschamps' grandmother, Suzanne Le Bouteiller.

The grant that Intendant Talon made to Deschamps was unlike most other grants made at the time with access to the St. Lawrence. It was not long and narrow, but wide and deep instead. It was still rectangular in shape, however, measuring six miles wide along the St. Lawrence and 4 ½ miles deep into the valley. The grant included land on both banks of a river that snaked its way through the property, a river that would also take on the name "Rivière Ouelle," or the Ouelle River.[2]

Boundaries were somewhat unclear in the early days of New France. The grant was considered to be large enough that exact boundaries did not really matter, although this ambiguity would eventually cause legal problems and court cases; a surveyor would have to be called in to set boundaries and settle lawsuits. The land to the west was also granted in 1672, but the land to the east of Deschamps' grant along the shores of

2 In order to avoid confusion, the distinction is being made between the seigneurie Rivière-Ouelle and the Ouelle River.

the St. Lawrence would only be granted after another two years. The land to the south of the grant was not conceded until many years later.

Deschamps' grant measured roughly 21,000 arpents, or 27 square miles of land, substantially larger than the grant mentioned by Asseline. It consisted mostly of densely packed evergreens and hardwoods, some marsh land at the mouth of the Ouelle River, and a fairly large peat bog to the east that covered about one-quarter of the property. The challenge for Deschamps was to bring in farmers to clear the forests and to plant and settle the land, under his agreement from the King; otherwise he risked forfeiting the grant.

With access to the St. Lawrence, the major communication link throughout the colony, with water supplied by the inland river, fertile soil, and plenty of wood for building and heating, Rivière-Ouelle, as it would be called interchangeably with La Bouteillerie, was a wise choice. The abundance of wild game and fish, including the porpoise and eel that would later contribute to Rivière-Ouelle's prosperity, made the property even more inviting. The absence of any permanent settlement of Amerindians, with only nomadic tribes coming to the river in the spring to hunt, fish, and eventually to trade, was an added attraction.

Internally the Ouelle River that originated up in the mountains to the south of the grant ran down through the property to the St. Lawrence, providing fresh water to much of the land and pushing back most of the salty influx from the St. Lawrence. It also provided transportation, connecting settlers on their own land grants with each other and with the St. Lawrence. Because the river's path took so many twists and turns, however, traveling within the seigneurie was challenging. There were (and still are) few places to easily cross it. Settlers had to use rafts or take their chances at lower tides.

If Deschamps had stood with his back to the St Lawrence and to the Laurentian Mountains far behind him on the river's northern shore, he could have looked out south over the vast expanse of forests across the valley to the hills far away over the land that comprised his new home. He surely must have been satisfied with his grant. While hopeful for the future, at least compared to what he might have had in France, he also knew the land came with significant responsibilities, if he was to fulfill his promise to the King. He could have stayed in Quebec, as many of his peers did, neglecting their grants, or taken an administrative post, but instead he was committed to living on and developing the land.

Little is known about what exactly Jean-Baptiste-François Deschamps de la Bouteillerie did during the year after his arrival, other than to begin work on his grant. He does appear to have been busy with that work. He chose the location of his home, away from the St. Lawrence and presumably its ice flows and perhaps bitter winter winds. He wrote a letter to his father shortly after arriving in Quebec and asked him to arrange to send over an additional woodworker. On October 29, 1671, he hired young Gabriel Lambert for five years at 90 livres a year to also help out on the estate. These actions would appear to confirm that he had already investigated and decided on a preferred grant site early on and was now scoping out the work involved.

Of course, obtaining a grant of land was one thing, but making it productive was another. Uncleared land in most parts of the colony was almost worthless. To grow the wheat that would become their livelihood took months and often years of hard work. The men had to cut down trees, remove branches, and clear the land of stumps. They would have used the better wood for homes and other structures and the rest for heating. Then they would have burned what was left on the ground, to add to the fertility of the soil. They also had to learn the fundamentals of farming since many of the men were artisans, not farmers. Most of them probably just followed the patterns and actions of earlier settlers, lessons that they must have learned sometime before arriving on the property.

While securing and starting work on his land grant, Jean-Baptiste must also have spent time looking for a wife. Perhaps his aunt had been making discrete inquiries among the upper classes in Quebec to find a proper woman for her noble nephew. Or perhaps other arrangements were being pursued by Deschamps or by his family in France. It's possible that even Intendant Talon might have helped out. Apparently,

Talon had taken notice of Deschamps' arrival and work. In November, 1671, after meeting Deschamps shortly after the young man's arrival in Quebec, Talon had written to the King's Minister of Finance Jean-Baptiste Colbert, commenting, in a slightly paraphrased passage, "If men of this quality come to Canada, we will have no problems colonizing New France."

Somehow the appropriate connections were made. A year after arriving in Quebec, having resolved the location of his land grant and having arranged for a home to be built on the property, Jean-Baptiste-François Deschamps de la Bouteillerie signed a contract to marry Catherine-Gertrude Macard on October 16, 1672. They were married eight days later in Quebec City.

Catherine-Gertrude was not quite 17 years of age at the time, having been born in Quebec on November 15, 1655. She had grown up in Quebec City and had spent two years from the age of ten at the nearby Ursuline School where she would have learned the fundamentals of the Catholic faith and the values of "honesty, humility, moderation, and curiosity." She would also have been taught "to read, write, do math, sew, and perform other activities appropriate to her sex."

She was the daughter of Marguerite Couillard, who had also been born in Quebec and who had deep family roots in New France. In fact, Catherine-Gertrude's great grandparents, Marie Rollet and Louis Hébert, were the first couple to establish a home in Quebec City less than a decade after its founding. Their daughter Guillemette had married Guillaume Couillard, who became a prominent figure in Quebec history. Guillaume and Guillemette had ten children, among them Marguerite, Catherine-Gertrude's mother.

In 1639, Marguerite had been married at the age of eleven to the Canadian explorer Jean Nicolet who had arrived in Quebec in 1618 from Cherbourg, at the tip of the Cotentin Peninsula, not far from where Jeanne was born twenty-five years later. Nicolet who apparently never learned to swim had died in a canoe accident crossing the rapids near Quebec City in October, 1642, leaving his French wife Marguerite with one child.

Four years after Nicolet's death, Marguerite had married again. Nicolas Macard, her second husband and Catherine-Gertrude's father, had been born around 1621 in Champagne, France. He had arrived in Quebec sometime in 1640 as an employee of the merchant company that was then in charge of the colony. He died when Catherine-Gertrude was only four years old, but not before fathering a total of six children with Marguerite.

Although the financial circumstances of Catherine-Gertrude's immediate family may have been stretched by the education of six children, as evidenced by the fact that her brother-in-law paid for her education, the wider Couillard family was a well-established family with significant financial resources. They would eventually be granted noble status in New France. The family would become community for Deschamps and Catherine-Gertrude; family members would be named godparents for their children.

Their marriage contract reflected the status of both families. It was executed at the home of Charles Bazire, a wealthy merchant and Deschamps' soon-to-be-brother-in-law. Like most marriages in upper class families, there was a significant exchange of property in the contract. Similar, as well, to marriages of this sort, it is difficult to determine whether it was a marriage of love or a smart alliance, or perhaps a mix of both. The Couillards gained a noble son-in-law and Deschamps gained an educated young bride, with solid and reputable family connections and financial resources. Reflecting Deschamps' wealth and status and perhaps the scarcity of such desirable young women with the proper upbringing, he gave his new bride a substantial gift of 10,000 livres. Catherine-Gertrude would also receive an annuity of 500 livres and a fixed sum of 3,000 livres upon Deschamps' death and before any division of their community property. As her contribution to the marriage, Catherine-Gertrude brought her trousseau of clothes, rings, jewelry, linens, her bedroom set and furnishings, and other personal belongings, valued at no less than 3,000 livres.

The contract signing which took place on October 16, 1672 must have been quite elaborate. Among those attending and signing the document were Comte de Frontenac, the newly appointed Governor of New France, Intendant Talon, Catherine-Gertrude's grandmother Guillemette Hébert, other members of the Couillard family, high society, and the new government, along with several officers of the recently disbanded Carignan Regiment. While Deschamps' father was still alive in France, his mother was listed as deceased on their marriage contract. His family might have been represented by his aunt although her presence has actually not been confirmed.

After their marriage in the church of Notre-Dame eight days later, Jean-Baptiste and Catherine-Gertrude almost certainly stayed in Quebec City until their home in Rivière-Ouelle was completed. Of course, Deschamps must have spent time on his grant, supervising the building of his home and the clearing of the land. On the 27th of September 1673, the couple's first son Jean-Baptiste-François was born and baptized in Quebec City, eleven months after their marriage.

The next year, on October 1, 1674, Jean-Baptiste contracted with Jacques Annets for one year of service to help with the seigneurie at a salary of 200 livres. He also began to make concessions of land to the men who had served out the terms of their three-year contracts with him and had demonstrated their commitment to settle in Quebec. Many of these men were countrymen from the same area in Normandy who had come with him in 1671. Among them were Robert Lévesque and Damien Bérubé.

Around this time, Jean-Baptiste and his wife Catherine-Gertrude must have moved into their new home in Rivière-Ouelle. Their next two sons Charles-Joseph and another Jean-Baptiste were, in all likelihood, born there, since there was a time interval between their births, in July 1674 and July 1676 respectively, and the registrations of their baptisms in Quebec City.

Few records exist to describe what their life was like in Rivière-Ouelle during those early years. It could not, however, have been very similar to the society living they would have had if they had stayed in Quebec City. If they were like other noble families residing on their land grants, their home was not very palatial and was probably built at least at first out of wood. By 1681, they apparently had at least one servant to help out with domestic chores.

Since Rivière-Ouelle was still an outpost at the time with few inhabitants, class lines could not have been all that rigid—at least in the beginning. As far as is known, there were no other non-native women living in Rivière-Ouelle until shortly after 1674 when the men who had received grants of land began to bring wives back to settle there. Only one other woman similar in rank to Catherine-Gertrude, Catherine Baillon, wife of Jacques Miville, would come to live in Rivière-Ouelle, and they did not arrive until around 1676. Prior to the arrival of other women, Catherine-Gertrude was probably busy getting their home settled, tending to their children, and visiting with relatives or friends in nearby seigneuries.

As the years passed, the Deschamps family continued to expand. A fourth son Henri-Louis was born to Catherine-Gertrude and Jean-Baptiste on February 7, 1679—this time, according to the registers, in Quebec City.

Jean-Baptiste and Catherine-Gertrude must have been quite happy to welcome new families to Rivière-Ouelle. Records provide evidence of their involvement in village activities, such as baptisms where they served as godparents for several children. Apparently, they did enjoy some symbols of respect due the nobility. While no official documents or journals exist from that time, there are stories of the traditional Maypole event on the first day of May. Rents and other levies were apparently paid at the Deschamps manor on St. Martin's Day, November 11. The family also would have had a special seat in the church when it was finally built and received special recognition during a church service or other village event.

7

Robert Lévesque

Church in Hautot-Saint-Sulpice

One of the first men to receive a grant from Deschamps, on November 10, 1674, was the carpenter Robert Lévesque. Lévesque had been baptized on September 3, 1642 in Hautot-Saint-Sulpice, a small Norman village in upper Normandy. He was the son of Pierre Lévesque and Marie Caumont who had married on October 27, 1641. His father died in May, 1648, and his mother in September, 1660, leaving Robert an orphan at 18 years old. When Robert sailed from France in 1671 on the same ship as Lord Deschamps, he left behind a brother, François, who had been baptized on April 5, 1644, and possibly other siblings.

While he was able to sign his name, his rough signature suggests that he had only rudimentary education, probably just enough to enable him to do his job as a carpenter. His ability to read is unknown. While there is a story that his father arranged for a carpenter's apprenticeship for Robert, the arrangement would have had to have been made at a very early age since his father died when Robert was seven years old. Somehow he did receive training. What is not known are his reasons for becoming a carpenter, whether, for example, he was following in his father's footsteps, or what attracted him to that profession. Among other unanswered questions are how he earned his living and whether he was a member of a carpenter guild, a requirement for many carpenters. The life of a carpenter could have been a good one. After all, Hautot-Saint-Sulpice at the time had 2,000 inhabitants, with a hospital, a church and several priests. However, it's also possible that he could have been an itinerant carpenter, which might not have been the easiest life, although perhaps better than farming.

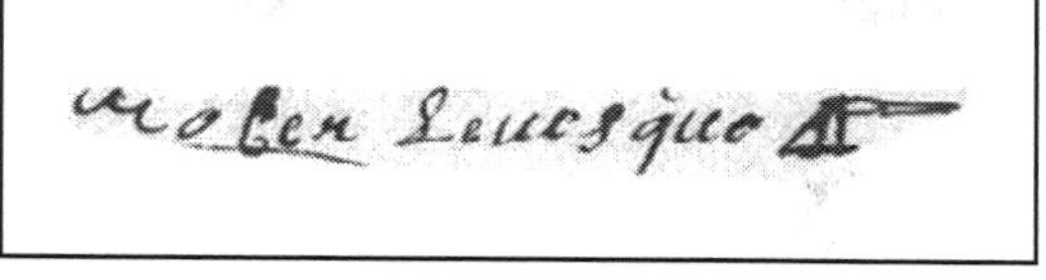

Signature of Robert Lévesque

His work probably led him to contacts with the Deschamps family. Since Hautot-Saint-Sulpice is only ten kilometers from the Deschamps home in Cliponville, it is quite possible that Robert had made Deschamps' acquaintance at a local market in nearby Yvetot, a great source of information, news and what today is called networking. Or perhaps Lévesque had built a solid reputation as a carpenter and Deschamps had sought him out to do some work for his family. Although they were similar in age, they probably did not socialize in the same circles.

Given the tenuous economic situation, his possibly questionable prospects in France at the time, and perhaps even his adventurous spirit, Robert would have listened with interest to Deschamps' story about opportunities in New France. Robert was one of those who signed up with Deschamps to leave his home in Normandy and seek his fortune in New France. In exchange for his voyage from France and the promise of some land, he had agreed to a three-year work engagement as a carpenter to help Deschamps build a home and clear the land on his estate in New France.

After fulfilling his contract, Robert received the promised grant from Deschamps, including the right to hunt and fish on the property. His grant, one of the two largest grants given out by Deschamps that year, was on the southern bank of the Ouelle River. Located directly across from Deschamps' estate, it encompassed 12 arpents of land on the south bank of the Ouelle River, spreading away from the river by 30 arpents deep, for a total of roughly two-thirds of a square mile. The size of the grant and its location suggests that he had become a good friend to Deschamps or had played a larger role than most of the others in building Deschamps' home. As a carpenter, along with helping Deschamps build his manor home, he must have built a small cabin for himself.

Like many other Frenchmen who arrived in those early decades of the colony, Robert did not have farming background, and therefore would have had to get used to the work required of him in New France. However, he also apparently decided to put his carpentry skills to work, something he was free to do once he had completed his contract with Deschamps. During the years from 1674 to1677, according to historian Ulric Lévesque, the rosters of workmen building *Le Petit Séminaire*, the Jesuit school for young boys in Quebec City, include Robert's name and provide information about his employment there. He was possibly involved in other building projects as well, along with continuing to clear his land in Rivière-Ouelle. It's also conceivable, as historian Lévesque suggested, that he had a friend help him with his clearing and planting work while he was in Quebec City performing more lucrative work.

By late 1678 he was an established carpenter, with a home and several arpents of cleared land, with shoes and clothes he had purchased, and with a suit he had had made from his salary from *Le Petit Séminaire*. But he was still single—at the age of 36. It was actually not all that unusual in 17th century France for young men of the lower classes to wait many years to marry. They needed to first build up some sort of financial foundation. Robert did not leave France until he was almost 29 years old. He spent the next seven years building that financial foundation for himself in his new mother country. But now, he needed to find a wife.

He was not alone in this predicament. At the time of their grants from Deschamps, most of the men were still single. Once they had their land secured, their next goal would have been to find a wife! But there were challenges. The *Filles du Roi* program had ended in 1673. Most of the 770 women who had come over as part of that program were married by 1674 and well on their way to having families four years later. The only other possibilities would be the small number of *Filles du Roi* who were still single, young widows, or the very few young women who were already in Quebec prior to 1663 when the *Filles Du Roi* program began, and who, for a variety of reasons such as age or class, would not be available to him.

Three of the men in Rivière-Ouelle were able to find wives and marry soon after they received their grants and were bringing them back to Rivière-Ouelle to start families. One of them, Jacques Thiboutout, a Cliponville native who had come over with Deschamps and Lévesque in 1671, had managed to find a wife, the twelve-year old daughter of a friend. Now that Robert had taken care of his financial situation, he too had to start his search.

How did he go about this search for a wife, in the age before newspapers, social media, or even the telephone? Like others in the same situation, such as Damien Bérubé, his neighbor and countryman from Normandy, he probably used his community of friends and colleagues to spread the word. At the time the number of people living in or around Quebec City and on the north and south shores of the eastern St. Lawrence River was still relatively small. With trading trips, work projects, and baptisms and weddings taking him to Quebec City, a young man such as Robert could have solidified friendships, particularly with compatriots from Normandy who spoke his native dialect. So he could have spread the word: "*Hard-working, single French male from Normandy, well positioned and respected carpenter, with a home, a farm, and good prospects, seeks wife. French-speaking widows with young children will be considered.*"

8

Robert and Jeanne

Lévesque succeeded in his quest, as did his friend Damien Bérubé a few months later. On April 22, 1679 36-year-old Robert married 35-year-old Jeanne Chevalier in L'Ange-Gardien. How he met Jeanne exactly is another mystery. To help him in his search for a wife, Robert could have asked friends, like Nicolas Paquin, to keep their eyes and ears out for available women. Paquin, another artisan from Normandy who had been sent over to New France by Deschamps' father, had worked with Robert in Rivière-Ouelle. He had left in 1675 and married a woman in Château-Richer, the village just next to L'Ange-Gardien where Jeanne was living with her first husband. With the small populations in both locations, it would not have been difficult for word to reach Robert about Jeanne's plight.

Another option is that Robert, in April 1677, attended a baptism in Quebec City for the child of a young couple from Rivière-Ouelle. It's quite possible that a family relative from L'Ange-Gardien was also attending the baptism. Back at home, that relative could have commented to her friends, including Jeanne, about the attractive bachelor. Or perhaps other friends in common, her LeTarte neighbors, for example, as Ulric Lévesque suggests, or other *Filles du Roi,* played a role. It's also conceivable that their paths could have crossed in Quebec City.

Another, very real possibility is that they had both been passengers on the same ship coming over to Quebec in 1671. Even if some sort of romantic spark had been ignited between them during the voyage, as has been suggested by at least one author, Robert would not have been able to marry in 1671. He first had to complete his three-year contract with Deschamps. And Jeanne would not have been able to wait for him to finish his contract since as a *Fille du Roi* she was obliged to marry as soon as possible, given the lack of real alternatives available to young respectable women in Quebec. However, they somehow could have managed to stay in touch.

Seigneur Deschamps might even have helped his friend Robert in his search. His wife's family owned land in L'Ange-Gardien. Although they resided in Quebec City, the family could have stayed connected with the settlers on their land. Upon hearing about Jeanne's tragedy, they could have passed on the news to relatives and friends. The possible connections were many.

Once Jeanne became "eligible" in late 1678 with Lecanteur's disappearance and once word spread, she probably had quite a few suitors—given the scarcity of women of marrying age at the time. Robert, somehow learning about Jeanne, could have visited with friends in L'Ange-Gardien and must have won out over any competition. Jeanne, left impoverished by Lecanteur, needed to find security. Even if she had noble origins and even if he did not have her first husband's refined presence and elaborate signature, Robert, with his more secure prospects, must have seemed a godsend. She apparently did not feel the need to wait two years or more, the normal interval for other widows after the death of their first husbands.

A marriage contract was drawn up. It was signed on April 21, 1679, a day before their wedding, in the company of their friends, including many from the LeTarte family in whose home the ceremony took place. Robert's parents are listed as the deceased Pierre Lévesque and the deceased Marie Caumont of Hautot-Saint-Sulpice, in the archdiocese of Rouen. The names of Jeanne's parents, now identified as being from St. Nicolas parish in the diocese of Coutances, raise questions. Her father was the "deceased Jean." The last name of her now deceased mother Marguerite, however, was actually left blank, but in the margin was written what looks like "Scorman," In later versions of the original contract, Marguerite's name has been transcribed as "Romain" or "Romian."

The contract recognized Jeanne's "dowry," without specifying any amount, her clothes, household linens and her other personal possessions, valued at thirty-six livres. These items were not to be considered community property, and none of these items was to be used to cover any debts incurred prior to their marriage. Jeanne had no home or inheritance to declare.

After promising to take each other as lawful husband and wife, they agreed to treat all their assets, except for those personal items belonging to Jeanne, as community property. Neither party was to have responsibility for any debts and mortgages incurred before their marriage. Robert agreed to support Jeanne's three sons who are named in the contract: Nicolas, Charles and the newborn Guillaume, until the age of twenty even though the normal obligation was only until the age of fifteen. He also transferred two arpents of land to François Boucher, his godson, son of a neighbor, presumably in recognition of some favor done to Robert by the neighbor. Ulric Lévesque has suggested that perhaps the father and son had been helping care for Robert's land in his absences while working in Quebec City or while searching for a wife!

Finally, the contract was signed by those who could, including Robert and Charles LeTarte.

Jeanne's marriage to Robert took place the next day, April 22, 1679, in her village of L'Ange-Gardien. The nine months that had elapsed after the birth of her son must have satisfied the authorities, as being within the interval set by convention for widows to remarry. Although no death certificate for Lecanteur has been found, the church must have been convinced by witnesses of his death since banns of marriage were published and the marriage was blessed by a priest.

In a separate document, Jeanne officially renounced her first husband's debts that day as well, as was her right as a widow. The land that Lecanteur had acquired had either already been returned to their owners or sold off by the court. The renunciation, executed by a notary, included an inventory of just over one page, detailing the property that remained from her marriage with Lecanteur. The value was now set at 46 livres, slightly more than specified in their marriage contract the day before.

***Justaucorps*[1]**

Thanks to historian Ulric Lévesque and one of the archivists in Quebec, it's possible to detail this property as consisting of a few pots and pans, an old brass pail, an axe, two old hoes, three old blankets, some household linens, and "five shirts belonging to [her] deceased [husband]." The inventory also listed a chest, or *coffre,* locked with a key and containing a *justaucorps,* an outer garment or waistcoat, usually somewhat elaborate, that must have been elegant enough to warrant being locked up. The rest of his clothes, according to the notary, "were mostly lost where he died or used to bury him."

Jeanne was left with only those few household items and her dowry. She did of course bring to the marriage her three young sons. Now Robert had an instant family. While the boys were extra mouths to feed, Nicolas at 6 ½ and Charles at 4 ½ years were fast approaching the age when they would be able to help Robert in the fields and in future clearing of more land on the farm.

Since Jeanne no longer had a home in L'Ange-Gardien, in all likelihood they moved her family quite soon after the wedding to a home that Robert would have built in Rivière-Ouelle during his eight years there. Since any existing roads were too muddy for travel, the trip to Rivière-Ouelle would have been by boat or raft. By late April, the ice on the St. Lawrence would have been breaking up because of the spring thaw that was actually mentioned in the wedding contract. Their most likely route would have been to sail from L'Ange-Gardien over to the

1 Courtesy of http://www.gentlemenoffortune.com/Justaucorps.htm

eastern tip of Île d'Orléans and then across the St. Lawrence to its southern shore, where wharves and stopping points were plentiful in those days. They would then have continued in a northeast direction, hugging the shoreline, until they reached the mouth of the Ouelle River.

It must have been quite a sight: Jeanne, Robert, a nine-month old baby and two young boys under the age of seven on a small raft, powered by a sail and oars. Were they alone or was there also a boatman on board to navigate the currents on the St. Lawrence? They did not have a lot to move, presumably, but there must have been some clothes and belongings and of course the few pots and other household items left from Jeanne's marriage to Lecanteur. Did she bring the five shirts from the inventory and the coffre with Lecanteur's coat inside? She actually might have done so since used clothes were as valuable as new ones! Was there anything else in that locked coffre that she might have brought with her to remind her of her life in France?

Jeanne must have had some mixed emotions. She was leaving behind neighbors in L'Ange-Gardien, located so close to Quebec City, along the fairly well populated Beaupré coast. The habitants in L'Ange-Gardien had even just built a church. Now she was moving her family far away from them. As they sailed along the river, she now might have noticed that farms and wheat fields had replaced some of those dense forests that she could have seen in her first view of this shore some eight years earlier. Here and there she might have also seen a small chapel and a few cabins. Nevertheless, it was still very much the "wild frontier."

What were the two older boys thinking as the raft finally turned south away from the St. Lawrence, and made its way around those many curves of the Ouelle River? How were they dealing with the change in fathers? In homes?

Within two years there would be a total of eleven families in Rivière-Ouelle. But when Robert brought Jeanne and her boys to their new home, the population would have been limited to Jean-Baptiste Deschamps, his wife and sons, three or four other families, and a small number of single men who were in various stages of settlement and finding wives. Homes and farm buildings would have been few and fairly spread out. There was no church, although presumably by 1679 the Deschamps' manor house would have been built.

Eventually, as more settlers and families arrived, Jeanne would have a new community. In fact, just a few months after Jeanne's arrival in Rivière-Ouelle, Damien Bérubé brought his new wife Jeanne Savonnet and her six children to join the other families. Bérubé's wife had arrived as a *Fille du Roi* a year before Jeanne and had also lost her husband in 1678.

Certainly for Jeanne and her young sons, the move must have been a jarring experience. Nevertheless, she might have just been relieved to have found some security through her marriage with Robert after what must have been unsettling years with Lecanteur. She might have been lonely at first, missing her friends in L'Ange-Gardien. As it turned out, she must have kept in touch with some of those folks over the decades to come. But for now, Jeanne had no choice except to set down new roots in Rivière-Ouelle. And she did, because she would live there for another 37 years.

9

Life on the south shore of the St. Lawrence River 1679–1688

For Jeanne and her family, their first dwelling in Rivière-Ouelle would have been the one that Robert had built sometime after his arrival in Quebec, close by the Ouelle River. Years later it was described as measuring 20' by 18', or 360 square feet, constructed like most homes of the time, according to one translation, "of roughly hewn logs stacked horizontally and secured by dovetail joints or vertical posts at the corners." The roof would have been steeply pitched to shed snow and rain and covered with overlapping boards. The floor would have been earthen, and it may or may not have been raised off the ground, although many homes were, to protect from the cold. There was no mention of a root cellar.

It was probably not a lot different from their home in L'Ange-Gardien, a single room with a stove and windows covered with oil skin, not glass. Their bed would have been in one corner. Her sons would have slept on the floor, on straw mattresses and covered in bear skins. As a carpenter, Robert would have made the cabin as snug as possible over the years and would probably have built a table with chairs or benches, a chest, or possibly an armoire, to hold kitchen items and personal belongings, and hopefully a cradle for the baby Guillaume. In another corner, rifles would have been stored, ready for warding off wild animals. Fortunately, they would not have been needed to fend off raids of Amerindians since the French colonists in the Rivière-Ouelle area managed to remain on somewhat friendly terms with the local native population. At some point, however, Jeanne probably did learn to shoot a rifle, as protection when Robert was away hunting or on carpentry projects.

As soon as they arrived in late April, 1679, Jeanne would have been busy, getting her sons settled and establishing new routines for them. It was late April and Robert may or may not have already planted a vegetable garden before leaving to marry Jeanne. Jeanne would have assumed responsibility for tending to it. Her days would have been filled with taking care of her children, preparing their food, and making or mending clothes, blankets and other household items. Most surely there were animals to be fed, cows to be milked, butter to be churned, eggs to be gathered, bread to be baked, and meat that Robert bought home to be cured. When they could, Jeanne and her sons would also have helped Robert out as he continued to clear, plant and harvest the fields or when he worked on the barn and stable. Since all their farm animals were sheltered there during the long winter months, walls of the barn had to be kept well insulated and ventilated to protect the animals from the cold and the spread of disease. Unquestionably, theirs was a tough and busy life.

And one that was certainly not glamorous. Though they were living in a cabin in the forest frontier, inside it was dark, dirty, and smelly, particularly during the long winters when the family would be cooped up inside. Jeanne would have used incense and herbs to mask the smells which could have been intense, from cooking and human bodies, including a young baby in diapers—without all the conveniences of 21st century living. There was no running water although the river was thankfully quite close by.

While in many respects her life in those early years in Rivière-Ouelle might have seemed a continuation of her days in L'Ange-Gardien, there were significant differences. In L'Ange-Gardien she had neighbors. There were close to 110 families living in the area at the time, compared to the less than ten families in Rivière-Ouelle. After eight years living in New France, Jeanne was probably used to the cold, to the winter, the too short spring, the busyness of summer, and the beauty of the fall. By now, she may have learned how to maneuver with snowshoes, to manage a birch bark canoe, and to use a toboggan to get around. Nevertheless, this was still wilderness. How did she deal with the isolation she would have encountered in Rivière-Ouelle?

Perhaps her new husband and three children left her no time to reflect on the situation. Still, compared to L'Ange-Gardien, there were more wild animals to fear, fewer neighbors to consult or with whom to share food and stories. Who would have been there to assist Jeanne with her children or with childbirth? To be sure, more frequent contact with Amerindians might have helped with adapting to the land around Rivière-Ouelle and with learning how to prepare meals with the meat of eels and porpoises, deal with ailments, and apply bear grease to herself and her children against the mosquitos and black flies. Nevertheless, if there was an accident, the nearest hospital and medical help were at least two days away.

The small community in Rivière-Ouelle in those first years must have established tight bonds. For a long time, there was no church, only a visiting priest who would have said mass, possibly once a month. Jeanne and her neighbors would have had to take the lead on teaching Bible stories and educating their children. A communal oven for baking bread and a mill for grinding wheat might have brought them together, but it is unclear when any of these appeared in the seigneurie.

Early on, their neighbors, of course, included Seigneur Jean-Baptiste-François Deschamps and his wife Catherine-Gertrude, whose home right across the river could bring some comfort and calm some of the fears Jeanne might have had any time Robert was away. When Robert, Jeanne, and her three sons arrived in Rivière-Ouelle, the Deschamps were most likely delighted to have Robert back with his new family. In addition to the work Jean-Baptiste had been doing to bring in more colonists to the seigneurie, their family was also growing. In early February, shortly before Jeanne and Robert arrived, Catherine-Gertrude had given birth to a fourth son, Henri-Louis, who would have been just six months younger than Jeanne's son Guillaume.

Jeanne's family with Robert soon started to expand as well. In early 1680, Jeanne gave birth to François-Robert. Because of the absence of a church in Rivière-Ouelle, Jeanne's newborn son was baptized in the home of his godparents, Seigneur Deschamps and his wife. It's possible that Catherine-Gertrude or another French or even Amerindian neighbor could have helped Jeanne with the birth and with her children.

The one-room cabin that Robert had built several years ago was surely becoming quite cramped, especially over the next few years with the addition of more children. At some point, he must have begun building a new one. They soon had a larger, half-timbered home that was over twice as large as their first home. It had two windows with glass panes and contained two rooms, one large one serving as a kitchen and family gathering space and another room, probably a bedroom, with a partially completed floor. An attic provided sleeping space for the children except perhaps during the cold winter months when they probably slept downstairs around the stove.

In the summer of 1681, two years after Jeanne's arrival in Rivière-Ouelle, the government of New France undertook a new census of the inhabitants of the colony. Unlike the earlier censuses that had only listed names and ages, the 1681 census was full of detail, including occupations, the number of cleared acres, rifles and even cattle (but apparently not including sheep, chickens and other farm animals). For Rivière-Ouelle, the 1681 census listed eleven families, all couples except for one widow, with 21 adults, 37 children, and 4 servants, for a total of 62 inhabitants. Those eleven households combined had 104 head of cattle and 31 rifles. Only cleared land was considered to have value; the 134 arpents of cleared land in Rivière-Ouelle compared favorably with surrounding seigneuries that were also starting to grow.

At the time of the 1681 census, Seigneur Deschamps, described as 37 years old, and his wife, age 24, had three children (ages seven, five, and three), three rifles, twelve head of cattle, and fifteen arpents of cleared land. They also had one servant, who was fifteen years old. For the Lévesque family, Robert was listed as 40 years old and Jeanne was 36. They had almost as much property as Deschamps: four rifles, ten head of cattle, and ten arpents of cleared land, but no servant.

Interestingly, one neighbor named Joseph Renaud, with his wife and her sister, and two "servants," had fourteen rifles, sixteen head of cattle, and fifty arpents of cleared land. Persistent research has uncovered the likely identity and story of this man. It appears he was a farmer and agent on land that was actually not part of Deschamps' seigneurie. Instead, Renaud was thought to be working for a neighboring seigneur, Charles Aubert de La Chesnaye, a wealthy financier and businessman who had been married to Catherine-Gertrude's sister before her early death. Renaud may have also been trading rifles for furs with the Amerindians on La Chesnaye's behalf.

According to the census, Jeanne's and Robert's family included only three sons: Nicolas and Charles Lecanteur, Jeanne's older sons from her first marriage, and now the newly born François-Robert. The youngest Lecanteur boy seems to have disappeared. He presumably had died sometime between their marriage in April, 1679 when he was mentioned and the middle of 1681, when the census was taken.

The census also did not list the first Deschamps son. No death certificate has been found for either child, possibly because Rivière-Ouelle did not have a permanent priest at the time. It is probably safe to assume, however, that they were no longer alive since no further mention of either child has been found.

Happily, at the time of the census, both Jeanne and Catherine-Gertrude were pregnant. Jeanne's second son with Robert, Pierre-Joachim, was born the following January. His baptism was recorded in the church in L'Islet, several kilometers down the road since the parish of Rivière-Ouelle was still not organized. Seigneur Deschamps' aunt, the nun Sister Saint Joachim from the *Hôtel-Dieu* in Quebec City, was named as his godmother.

Catherine-Gertrude, Deschamps' wife, was not as fortunate in her pregnancy as Jeanne. On November 21, 1681, she died, after having given birth to their last son, Jean-François, just a few days after her 26th birthday. Her baby son died with her. The attending priest registered their deaths in L'Islet, although Catherine-Gertrude and her son were buried on land that would eventually become Rivière-Ouelle's first cemetery. Her grandmother Guillemette Hébert survived her by three years, dying at the age of 78; her mother Marguerite Couillard outlived her youngest daughter by 24 years.

Since their first son had not lived long enough to be in included in the 1681 census, Deschamps would have been left with three young sons at the time of his wife's death: seven-year-old Charles-Joseph, five-year-old Jean-Baptiste-François, and three-year-old Henri-Louis. It would have been difficult to raise his sons in Rivière-Ouelle without a wife to keep his home and care for his children, particularly at a time in history with rigid roles for men and women.

According to Paul-Henri Hudon, the prominent Canadian historian, in keeping with the custom of the time, the sons would have been sent to live with their godparents who would serve as guardians until the boys came of age. Those families, members of the established Couillard family and Catherine Gertrude's relatives, lived in Quebec City. They thus would have been able to raise the boys to the "noble way of life," ensuring they received the proper education at the seminary or in military academies and learned appropriate manners, postures, dress and speech. Their father would not have been able to arrange such a suitable upbringing because he was occupied with developing the seigneurie far from Quebec City. He was, however, responsible for paying for their schooling.

The frequency of Deschamps' visits with his sons is another unknown in this man's life, whether they came to Rivière-Ouelle to visit, whether they got together on his trips to Quebec City, or many other details of their early lives. But one thing that is definitely known is that Deschamps remained single for almost 20 years after his wife died, a rare occurrence that deserved mentioning in at least one Canadian history book.

***

After his wife's and son's deaths in 1681 and with his three surviving sons living in Quebec City with relatives, Deschamps concentrated on developing Rivière-Ouelle in order to fulfill his agreement with the

King. He reportedly spent most of his time on his seigneurie, leaving it only for occasional trips to Quebec City for baptisms, other events, or visits with friends and family.

There are stories of Deschamps, dressed in a nobleman's finery, with his sword at his side, receiving dues and rents in the family manor, while seated at a table covered with a fine tapestry cloth. While these stories may or may not be true, he does seem to have been a responsible, and perhaps quite generous, landlord. He made several more concessions of land to newcomers that included the right to fish which would later turn out to be a rather prosperous privilege for them. In the spring of 1684 he ceded part of his own estate to be used for a church and cemetery. The agreement was later confirmed by Jeanne's husband Robert Lévesque and another vestry member. Since thirty families were usually needed to justify a church and Rivière-Ouelle still fell short of that number at the time, this decision was a bold step and one that would have been sanctioned by the Bishop in Quebec City.

A wooden church was built and its registers were opened in January of 1685. All the work was completed by the inhabitants of the seigneurie. Robert Lévesque, as carpenter, would have played a significant role in those projects. It's not known if this chapel had a seigneurial pew for Deschamps and his family, although a church that replaced it several years later certainly would have had one.

Finally, Rivière-Ouelle had a church and a priest to provide the inhabitants with regular services and a consistent religious presence. In addition, the church, as in other parishes, served as a social gathering place for celebrations of weddings, feast days and other special events. It would help build a sense of community against the isolation of the frontier and allow for meeting future spouses. It also provided a place for the exchange of news and information.

In addition to dealing with his family tragedies and seigneurial projects, Deschamps' life as seigneur of Rivière-Ouelle had other challenges—both legal and financial. In 1675 boundary disputes began with his neighbor in Grande Anse (also known as La Pocatière), just to the west of Rivière-Ouelle, disputes that were not completely resolved until thirteen years later. In 1676, he was involved in a law suit, over a question of responsibility for a bad container of salted fish, a suit he apparently lost.

In 1685, a new law in Quebec officially allowed nobles to engage in commerce. Deschamps had apparently already been taking advantage of this opportunity. In 1684, twenty residents of the south coast of the St. Lawrence, including Deschamps, Jeanne's husband Robert Lévesque, and their neighbor, Aubert de La Chesnaye, now seigneur of nearby Kamouraska, sent a request to the King to protest the withdrawal of what they considered their rights to hunt, fish and trade with the First Nation peoples. The suit appears to have resulted in a compromise settlement. It's quite possible that Deschamps initiated other business ventures and faced several other legal issues. The lack of documents, lost or destroyed over time, and the prevalence of verbal agreements, never officially documented, leave this possibility an open question.

Deschamps' attempts to grow his estate obviously took effort. In addition to these legal matters, he had to recruit families to relocate to Rivière-Ouelle, provide them with grants, and hope that they would in turn recruit additional settlers who would all expand his revenue base. Apparently this hope was realized, as records listed the arrival of fifteen new families between 1681 and 1690. Most of these families came from L'Ange-Gardien, Château-Richer, and other places near Quebec City where Jeanne and other founding settlers had lived. They must have been able to spread the word about greater opportunities for land away from the areas around Quebec City that were becoming more crowded and where land for future generations was becoming scarce. A few spouses and even families also arrived from France.

These settlers may have expected to find a communal mill on the property since this was usually an attraction, as well as a seigneurial responsibility and source of revenue for the seigneur. In Rivière-Ouelle, however, a seigneurial mill did not appear until 1709. Problems apparently arose over finding a proper location for such a structure any earlier than that and having enough residents to justify the expense of building and maintaining a mill. Smaller mills, owned by one of the habitants, may have taken the place of a larger one. According to custom, Deschamps would have had to approve such mills and could have confiscated them or demanded part of the revenue from them, but it is not known if he ever exercised these rights.

Growth of the estate also demanded financial resources from Deschamps. Money appears to have been a problem although no budgets or records exist to confirm the situation. More than likely, revenues from the seigneurie or any help from his family in France were not as expected, and the costs to develop the seigneurie, maintain a manor, and pay for his sons' educations were higher than anticipated since he evidently needed more financial support. In 1677, upon the death of his father, he asked his sister Anne to inquire as to whether there was any inheritance coming to him (there apparently was none.) The following year, he had to secure a loan of 800 livres from the *Hôtel-Dieu* where his aunt resided and then another one two years later, for 3,724 livres from his brother-in-law, François Prevost, a wealthy merchant in Quebec City. There may have been other loans as well that were not recorded. He also apparently failed to pay Nicolas Paquin, the Norman countryman whom his father had recruited years earlier, the sum of 180 livres that was due Paquin for his contracted engagement.

In spite of these challenges, growth in Rivière-Ouelle continued. And in Jeanne's family as well. On December 11, 1684, another son, this one named Joseph, was born. His baptism, held in January, 1685, was the one of the first baptisms to be registered in the parish records in the newly erected church of Rivière-Ouelle. His godfather appears to have been Joseph Renaud, their neighbor who may have then been living in Rivière-du-Loup, where his business with La Chesnaye was apparently located.

Over the next few years, Rivière-Ouelle, in its isolated location, was relatively untouched by political events taking place in the rest of North America, extensions of battles in Europe between France and her enemies Spain and England, that spread to New France where they were joined by their First Nation allies. Although the settlers in Rivière-Ouelle seem to have remained at peace with their own First

Nation neighbors and were spared the fighting, they unfortunately did not remain untouched by epidemics. An epidemic in 1688 of smallpox and measles killed over 1,000 inhabitants in all of New France, close to 10% of the population. In Rivière-Ouelle, nine deaths were recorded between December 1687 and the middle of March, 1688.

In Jeanne's and Robert's home, the epidemic brought double tragedy. In December 1687, their fourth son, 14-month-old Jean-Baptiste, died. Two months after his death, another son, also named Jean-Baptiste, was born, but only survived for a month.

The epidemic additionally claimed Jacques Miville and his wife Catherine Baillon, one of the first women to arrive in Rivière-Ouelle. Damien Bérubé and Jacques Thiboutout, two of Deschamps' and Robert's countrymen who had come over on the ship with them, also died. It must have been a particularly sad time for Jeanne, Robert, Deschamps, and the other early settlers.

10

Life on the south shore of the St. Lawrence River 1689–1699

The community eventually recovered, but two years later it was met with another challenge, this time quite a different one, caused by those wars begun in Europe by Louis XIV that had spread to the British colonies south of Quebec. In apparent retaliation for incursions by the French into those colonies, Britain sent a fleet of 32 ships with two thousand soldiers, commanded by Sir William Phips. The ships appeared in the eastern part of New France in 1690. They first wreaked havoc on Acadia (later known as Nova Scotia) and then afterward, in early October 1690, showed up off the shores of Rivière-Ouelle. Their presence produced a tale that has been told and retold, in Rivière-Ouelle at least, often with embellishments and not without confusing facts. Here is a brief summary of the events.

According to the "Annals of the Hôtel-Dieu" in Quebec City, villagers along the south shore of the St. Lawrence were warned of the fleet's arrival and its intention of taking Quebec and of attacking small villages on their route. The settlers in Rivière-Ouelle were thus prepared when Phips sent six ships to their shores, loaded with 25 men each. Led by the parish priest, forty "heroes" managed to defend Rivière-Ouelle and send the British soldiers on their way to Quebec City. Phips met defeat there at the hands of the French in mid-October and went back home. Life returned to normal along the river.

The names of those who participated in defending Rivière-Ouelle have been repeated through the years, only to be challenged by recent research. Robert Lévesque and his two Lecanteur sons were definitely part of the defense of Rivière-Ouelle. Two of Deschamps' sons were originally listed as participants, possibly incorrectly, according to analysis of more recent information about ages and school records.

The whereabouts of Seigneur Deschamps remains a mystery as well, since he was not listed as participating in the rout in Rivière-Ouelle. His aunt, Sister St. Joachim, died in May 1690 in Quebec City. Did he attend her funeral? Did he perhaps stay in Quebec City and then end up helping to defend the government? Or had he possibly returned to France? No records of any land transactions or other registered appearances of Deschamps have been found from April 1689 to early 1692.

Absence of such records has led one historian to speculate. He wonders whether Deschamps might have returned to France sometime in 1689 to share the news of births, marriages, and deaths with his family and those of his Norman countrymen and to visit with his remaining siblings and with one of his sons who was pursuing a military career there. It's also possible that Deschamps went back to France to seek financial help since in 1688 his brother-in-law had decided to sue him for payment of that 3,724 livre loan made eight years earlier. To date, none of these hypotheses has been confirmed.

With or without Seigneur Deschamps' presence for those years, Rivière-Ouelle continued to experience change and growth. Along with other families, Robert and Jeanne continued to prosper. Their family farm was growing, helped along by their sons. Once the boys turned eight or nine, they would have been old enough to work with Robert in the fields and to help him build their new home to house the growing family. Thus, by late 1690, the two Lecanteur sons along with Jeanne's two older sons with Robert would have already been out in the fields, helping their father clear and plough the land and harvest the wheat. Only Joseph who was not quite six would have remained at home with Jeanne. With that sort of assistance, the farm could have expanded quite rapidly. The family now also owned a narrow strip of uncleared land on the shores of the St. Lawrence that Deschamps had granted Nicolas Lecanteur, Jeanne's oldest son, in 1689. The reasons for this gift remain unclear, but it certainly added to the Lévesque/Chevalier property.

In addition to the increased land acreage, the family fortunes appeared to have been improving significantly. On August 11, 1692 Robert and Jeanne were able to purchase three parcels of cleared and uncleared land from their neighbor and friend Joseph Renaud, who had been accumulating land in Rivière-Ouelle through grants from Deschamps or by buying land from other settlers. The purchase included a house, barn and stable, and tripled the amount of land that Jeanne and Robert owned. Presumably Robert was being paid for carpentry projects by neighbors or those habitants further away because they were able to quickly pay off the purchase price of 2,200 livres within two years.

The purchase of this large grant of land was most certainly made to eventually provide property for their sons. Shortly after the purchase, on September 25, 1692, Jeanne and Robert made the first gift of some land from this purchase to Nicolas, Jeanne's oldest son. Unfortunately, he died, of unknown causes, just over a month later. This grant was annulled the next year. Charles, Jeanne's remaining Lecanteur son, received a grant of part of this land from Jeanne and Robert six years later, in October 1698. The land that Deschamps had given to Nicolas in April, 1689 remained in the family.

Meanwhile, their attempts to grow their family had brought sorrows. In the fall of 1690, at the time of the Phips raid, Jeanne, who was then 47 years old, had another child. Finally they had a daughter, Marie-Anne, born October 3, 1690. Sadly, she died ten days later. Thus in the span of almost five years, from January 1686 until October 1690, Jeanne was pregnant, and for the last four years of that period, she was delivering and then burying three infants. How did she deal with those losses—a grief experience that was shared by many other families throughout New France in those early days in the colony? It's not difficult to imagine the pain although it has been suggested that women were prepared to deal with these losses because of the frequency of early deaths.

Fortunately, for other families and for the future of Rivière-Ouelle, babies did survive. Children grew up. They married sons and daughters of other Rivière-Ouelle settlers or their friends and then settled down in Rivière-Ouelle, with their expanding families. Families also continued to arrive in Rivière-Ouelle from elsewhere in Quebec and from France. Another twenty families were added to the rosters of Rivière-Ouelle during the years 1690 to 1703. In 1694 a larger church replaced the wooden chapel that had been built nine years earlier.

While the English colonies south of Quebec were caught up in Salem Witch trial hysteria in 1692, records show that Deschamps had resumed making grants to several new settlers that year. In the same year, he also ceded his manor to the church to be used as a residence for the new priest. There are no records of or references to a new manor being built during his lifetime. What appears most reasonable is that he then moved into the house on the land that Robert and Jeanne had just purchased from Joseph Renaud. If that move in fact did happen, he presumably would have brought his domestic servant to handle day-to-day housekeeping chores for him. The new location would have become the estate's manor for payment of taxes and settlement of any local matters.

Besides encouraging new settlers and moving his residence, Deschamps continued to explore other avenues for growth and prosperity for Rivière-Ouelle. On 11 May, 1697, Governor Frontenac conceded to Jean-Baptiste-François Deschamps de La Bouteillerie and two other men fishing rights on the *Iles des Pelerins*, islands located in the St. Lawrence almost 39 kilometers further northeast of Rivière-Ouelle. Apparently these three were planning some sort of fishery to take advantage of the growing demand for the skin, oil and meat of porpoises. He also hired a notary to serve the community and act as captain of the militia as well. Presumably the additional families were generating enough revenues in the seigneurie for Deschamps to fund these projects.

By 1698 Rivière-Ouelle had a population of 105 men, women and children. According to a survey done 11 years later at the King's request, "the lands were quite beautiful and the residents were well off." The growth compared favorably with other nearby settlements, although exact comparisons are not easy. But it was still a frontier outpost, since that year there were 15,355 people living in New France, with much larger concentrations around Quebec City, Montreal and Trois-Rivières.

***

In the final year of the 17th century, only one of Jeanne's sons with Lecanteur was alive along with her three surviving children with Robert. Charles was close to twenty-five years old, François-Robert was 19, Pierre-Joachim was 17 and Joseph two years younger. Despite the grief from the loss of five children and the toll that hard work must have taken on them, Jeanne and Robert could have been ready to face a new century with a sense of satisfaction.

Not only did they have a more substantial home, they also now had a large farm that was thriving. In fact, they were one of the most prosperous families in the area. They had land for their sons and now owned two houses, a stable, a barn and several farm animals on their own property. In addition, they now owned the Renaud land that included a home and farm buildings. Robert was a leader in the village of Rivière-Ouelle, having played a major role in fighting off the English in 1690, serving as a church warden, and having helped in the construction of the new church. Based on the inventory of their possessions that would be made three years later, their home was comfortably furnished, with beds, linen, a table and chairs, other furniture, possibly some even imported from France, dishes, bowls, pewter kitchenware, and other household and personal items. And their relationship, even if at first it had been based on economic necessity, by now would have, at the very least, evolved into strong affection and mutual respect, if not love.

Jeanne would have played a large role in their success, although her contributions may not have been recognized by historians. Like all the women in rural New France at the time, she would have helped her husband in his work in the fields, tended to the family garden, fed the livestock, kept her family fed and clothed, including baking a multitude of loaves of bread every week, all while watching over their children when Robert was otherwise occupied with his carpentry work. Jeanne would have had to do all this on her own, without any help from daughters since her only daughter had died in 1690.

Life was undoubtedly quite different with Robert from what she had known with her first husband. There was more routine and structure, more time to enjoy life, socialize with neighbors, and even get dressed up for celebrations when Robert could wear a fancy *justaucorps* and Jeanne could don a new dress. And they certainly enjoyed much more security. Jeanne might even have helped Robert manage the farm and his carpentry business! According to at least one historian, there is some evidence that men concluded nothing of consequence without consulting their wives. While that may not have been true with Lecanteur, Jeanne might indeed have played a more active role in decision-making with Robert.

They must have built a strong community, with close friends including the Deschamps family and others from Jeanne's home in L'Ange-Gardien. This community, particularly the women, Jeanne among them, certainly played a role in passing on traditions, new and old, stories from the Bible, or from Normandy and other regions in France. They all would have helped newcomers and each other adapt to the nuances of living in Rivière-Ouelle, creating new traditions, merging songs, recipes, dialects, and customs.

Did Jeanne and Robert stop and think about what their lives would have been like if they had stayed in France? Perhaps it would have been less primitive and free of the snows and ice of winter. However, in New France at least they had their independence and with each passing year, a future that was more and more promising. Their lives were relatively free from disease, and taxes were quite low. They had clean air and water and plenty of fresh food. They had been spared the damages and perturbations caused by the fighting between Catholics and French Huguenots in France. They had avoided the consequences of the battles with France's enemies, including the 1694 destruction of Dieppe, that finally led to the Treaty of Ryswick in 1697. And they had avoided the suffering from poor harvests and major epidemics that plagued France during much of the last decades of the 17th century.

However fortunate they may have felt, life would take some unexpected turns. Another epidemic did strike Rivière-Ouelle in 1699 and took its toll on the Lévesque family and Rivière-Ouelle.

Part Four

Rivierè-Ouelle 1699-1716

Beginning again and saying good-bye

11

Beginning again 1699–1701

The epidemic that spread throughout New France in 1699, like the one eleven years earlier, did not leave Rivière-Ouelle untouched. This time it was either influenza or yellow fever. By the end of the year eleven people had died. Among the dead was Robert Lévesque, Jeanne's husband of more than twenty years. Robert died on September 11, 1699 less than two weeks after his 57th birthday. Twenty five days later, Charles, Jeanne's second son with Lecanteur and the last to survive his father, died at the age of 24.

Jeanne was now a widow, for the second time. She was 56 years old.

When Robert died, Jeanne faced a very different future from the one she had faced twenty years earlier. At his death, Robert was a successful farmer and carpenter, a hero of the Phips Raid, as well as a leader in the community. Jeanne and Robert had managed to purchase land, with funds presumably from Robert's carpenter trade and the work of their sons on the farm. Together she and Robert had built a farm that by 1699 included three homes with furniture and furnishings, several farm buildings, and a large number of farm animals. Their property encompassed over 1200 acres of land, one of the largest properties in Rivière-Ouelle.

By law Jeanne received one-half of the property she and Robert had accumulated. The remaining half belonged to her three surviving sons who had not yet reached the age of majority—twenty-five years at the time. Because of her sons' age, tutors were named to manage their shares of the estate.

Jeanne even had property of her own. The slice of land along the St. Lawrence that Seigneur Deschamps had granted in 1689 to Nicolas, her first born son with Lecanteur, had passed to his brother Charles when Nicolas died. Upon the death of Charles, Jeanne, as his next of kin, had inherited that piece of land as well as the land that Jeanne and Robert had given to Charles.

As a widow, Jeanne had more independence than she had had as a married woman since widows enjoyed full rights according to the Law of Paris and were no longer under marital or paternal authority. Given the fact that legally widows could become active outside the home, Jeanne's choices now, with grown children, were far more appealing than they had been twenty years earlier. With more security and freedom than ever before, did she ever consider leaving Rivière-Ouelle and moving closer to Quebec City? Undoubtedly the ties with her family and her friends, nurtured over the past twenty years, made leaving Rivière-Ouelle difficult, if not impossible?

This time surely there was no need to marry again. But she did.

12

Jeanne's third marriage

On April 5, 1701, eighteen months after Robert's death, Jeanne married Jean-Baptiste-François Deschamps, Seigneur de la Bouteillerie. There was no contract of marriage, only a registration in the parish records, listing their ages and parents and a waiver of any banns. This time, Jeanne's parents are listed as Jean Chevalier and Marguerite Scormand, both deceased. Jeanne was 57 years old. Deschamps was said to be 55 and his parents were Lord Jean Deschamps and Elizabeth DeBin, also both deceased. No documents have been found to explain why they decided to marry or why he had waited 20 years to marry again, longer than just about all the other men of his class.

There are many possible ways to explain Deschamps' long celibacy. They range from guilt and long-enduring grief over losing his wife at such a young age to the inability to find someone appropriate, to his tenuous financial situation that would have made supporting a new family difficult. Or perhaps he was too busy building the seigneurie and had no time to find and pursue a mate. There is also the possibility that he might have had a secret love, although that idea has been dismissed. Rivière-Ouelle was so small a place and the Catholic religion so strong, that such an illicit relationship was probably not tenable.

Imagining, creating, or writing a beautiful love story between Jeanne and Deschamps is also an option that helps explain his long-term celibacy and perhaps Jeanne's decision to marry again. Assuming the distinct possibility that Jean-Baptiste and Jeanne had indeed arrived from France in 1671 on the same ship, they could have met on board.

Jeanne could have had some training as a nurse and had been called up to help minister to a crew member or even to Deschamps himself for some injury. Deschamps might have taken notice of her, but any attraction would have been quickly extinguished because of the class differences at the time. When they met again in 1679, upon Jeanne's arrival in Rivière-Ouelle with Robert, they were both married. When Deschamps' wife died in 1681, Jeanne was still married. But finally, when Robert died in 1699, they could marry. They just had to wait a respectable amount of time.

This version, of course, does not take into account Jeanne's long and apparently successful, even loving, marriage with Robert. Fortunately, there are more practical, less romantic explanations. Over the years, as Robert's and Jeanne's farm grew and they became more prosperous and as the passage of time in New France broke down class barriers—at least in the countryside, they might all have settled into a life as neighbors and good friends. Thus, at the end of 1699, after Robert's death, Jeanne and Deschamps were two old friends, now both without a spouse, facing lonely years ahead. At that point they could have decided they did not want to face growing old alone. It is also possible that he was ill and needed someone to take care of him.

Historian Ulric Lévesque has offered an even more logical, and definitely less romantic, theory around their decision to marry although it does not really explain Deschamps' long-term bachelorhood. According to Ulric, when Deschamps gave his manor in the spring of 1692 to the church to be used as a home for the priest, he needed a place to live. There is no evidence that he built another manor. Given what appears to have been his fragile financial situation, he could have moved into the house that had come with the Renaud land purchase that Jeanne and Robert made a few months after he gave his home to the church. He could have lived there with François-Robert, the oldest of the Lévesque sons who at 19 might have been ready to move out of the family home where he was living with his parents and brothers into his own space. By 1701, however, François-Robert was 21 and had found a woman to marry. They needed a home of their own. Deschamps could have moved into the little cabin that had been Robert's first home, but perhaps Jeanne's home was a more appealing place to live. There was not a lot of available housing, as there is now. However, moving in with Jeanne required that they marry—in the 17th century at least.

Of course, these more logical conjectures do not address the reasons why Jeanne chose to marry again, giving up her newly acquired independence and status as head of the family. Nor do they explain why Deschamps waited so long to re-marry.

Whatever their reasons for marrying, they did. Deschamps moved into the house where Jeanne had lived with Robert, as evidenced by later documents that mentioned his residence there. She was now "Madame de la Bouteillerie," a title reserved for commoners who married into nobility. As a commoner, apparently, she could not assume the title of "la Seigneuresse," as his first wife had.[1]

What was her new life like? It must have meant at least some sort of change for her. After all, their home became the manor house of the seigneurie. Even if Deschamps by then had given up any pretense of nobility and become more like just any other upscale habitant, he still had responsibilities. Rents needed to be collected, and minor administrative problems needed to be resolved. He could have hired a manager, but there is no indication that he did.

No record exists as to how their families reacted. Jean-Baptiste still had sisters living in France. Did he write them and let them know? What sort of response did he receive? And what about his sons? By 1701 his oldest son Charles-Joseph was 27 years old and soon to be ordained as a priest in Quebec. His second surviving son was in the military in France. His third son Henri-Louis, who would eventually inherit the estate, was 22 years old and was also building a successful career in the military.

And what about Jeanne's sons? How did they feel about their mother marrying a nobleman, less than two years after the death of their father? There is no evidence that they had approved or were

---

1 This is the final argument that Jeanne did not come from a noble family since if she had had noble origins, she could have taken the title "la Seigneuresse."

asked to give permission or be witnesses to the marriage, all steps that they may have felt were their right. There is some evidence, however, that there were problems with at least one of her sons, although the cause cannot be tied directly to her remarriage. Such conflict within families was said to be common in those days (apparently little has really changed in that regard!). It's possible her sons were chaffing at having another new authority in their lives. Although they still had their guardians, Deschamps would have more responsibility since he would by law become head of household.

As was the custom in New France upon a spouse's remarriage, an inventory of Jeanne's and Robert's community property was drawn up and executed in March, 1702. This inventory was decidedly different from the one completed in April, 1679, when Jeanne renounced the debts of her first husband. This time, two days were required to complete the eleven-page inventory. Compared to other similar inventories of the time, the property that Jeanne and her sons inherited at Robert's death was quite substantial.

Included in the property were two houses on the Lévesque/Chevalier land, a barn and a stable, eight cows, a heifer, two young calves, eight bulls, four of whom were considered large work oxen, and pigs. Inside the houses, the inventory included cooking utensils, a pepper mill, bowls, dishes, tableware, an oval table, six chairs, tablecloths, napkins, sheets, other linen, armoires and several *coffres* or chests, two of which could be locked with a key. Perhaps one of the two coffres remained from her marriage with Lecanteur and had contained Lecanteur's elegant *justaucorps*?

The master bed, with its down mattress, one green and one white blanket from Normandy, pillows and a "tower" of green serge, was not included. It was undoubtedly a more elaborate bed than one would expect to find in an average habitant's home. Most likely it was Deschamps' bed which he brought with him to their home since the bed was not counted in the value of Jeanne's and Robert's belongings. It was mentioned in the inventory simply to acknowledge its existence.

The inventory listed another feather bed, quilts, sheets, and blankets, several yards of different sorts of fabric, which according to Ulric Lévesque, would mostly have been used for clothing, undergarments, and possibly sails. Jeanne still had three sons to clothe, and as grandmother, she would also be making clothes for her future grandchildren. Some of the nicer fabric could have been accumulated to make handsome shirts for upcoming nuptials.

Jeanne's personal belongings and clothes and those of her sons were not included in the inventory. However, Robert's personal belongings were listed. They included twelve shirts, a pair of boots, two pairs of shoes, a coat and finally three *justaucorps*, each of which was valued at eighteen livres. Could one of them have belonged to Jeanne's first husband?

Finally, there were six old rifles and an old carabine (worth 50 livres!), a large assortment of carpentry tools, farm implements, fishing equipment, seventeen beaver skins, a barrel of lard, a large supply of wheat, and some pine planks.

The very detailed listing came to a total value of more than 5,630 livres. According to the inventory, Jeanne had 306 livres in currency on hand. She was owed 470 livres, of which she considered 68 livres to be uncollectible. She owed a total of 122 livres to the church in Rivière-Ouelle and to a neighbor. In addition, there was the land from Robert's original grant and also from the Renaud purchase 1692. The total value came to over 8,000 livres, as compared to the less than 50 livres left from Jeanne's marriage to Lecanteur. The new inventory did not include the value of the land that Deschamps have given to Jeanne's first son because it now belonged solely to her.

At the time of the inventory, Jeanne's three sons wanted to come to some arrangement about the property since they were getting older and presumably pursuing the possibility of marriage. In fact, in November, 1701, seven months after his mother married Deschamps, François-Robert had married Marie-Charlotte Aubert, the daughter of a well-situated family on the Beaupré coast, along the northern shore of the St. Lawrence.

Thus, three days after the inventory was completed, Jeanne made an agreement with her sons for a division of the property, including her share of the community property. The arrangements were to be temporary, to remain in effect "during the life of said lady only." Jeanne retained the right to sell any of the property. In the agreement with her sons, François-Robert, the oldest, gave up his share of the inheritance. In exchange, he received 493 livres and land from the Renaud purchase, which included the house where he and his new wife were living. He also promised to spend a week annually working for his mother, chopping wood or taking wheat to the mill, just not during harvest time.

In addition to this agreement with all three sons, Jeanne concluded a five-year business arrangement and lease with her second oldest son, Pierre-Joachim, to manage her share of the community property. The arrangement included a promise to share the produce from this land and a commitment to keep the property profitable. He did not receive any right to sell the property.

The reasons for her choice of Pierre-Joachim over her oldest son François-Robert were not documented. It appears that she might not have been on the best of terms with François-Robert. The notary in the inventory conducted three days earlier had noted that he had taken 163 pounds from the estate that he did not want to account for or return. He had also sold eleven wood planks from the inventory of goods for his own benefit. It is unclear why he took these actions. Historian Ulric Lévesque suggests that perhaps he felt he was due a larger share of the land as the eldest in the family, although French law at the time did not recognize any such rights. Perhaps he was jealous of the special land arrangements that Jeanne had made for her Lecanteur sons. Or he might have been upset by his mother's remarriage less than two years after his father's death, to a nobleman who was also his godfather.

A week after the agreements were signed, Pierre-Joachim requested and received emancipation from having a guardian. While the document does not make clear what might have precipitated this decision, the choice of Pierre-Joachim to manage Jeanne's half of the property could explain the decision. He probably felt he needed more freedom to make decisions without having to confer or get approval from his guardian or his step-father. Or there might indeed have been friction with his older brother, who was trying to assert his role as "head of household."

It is also not clear who was running Deschamps' estate at this time, whether Deschamps was still active or whether he had brought in a manager. On April 8, 1702, a year after his marriage to Jeanne, he did sell his share of the Pelerin Isles to a merchant from Quebec City. A week later, he would have attended his oldest son's ordination to the priesthood on the 15th of April in Quebec City. His strong signature on documents executed during this time would seem to argue that he was still in good health.

Socially, the new couple was quite active. On November 29, 1702, Jeanne's first grandchild was born to François-Robert and Charlotte Aubert. Marie-Jeanne Lévesque was baptized the next day. Jeanne and her new husband were named as the baby's godparents. Notarial records indicate they were also attending baptisms, in Rivière-Ouelle and perhaps Quebec City, and serving as godparents to other children as well.

The first few years of the new century were promising. Slow but steady growth continued in the population of Rivière-Ouelle, through births of new children, new marriages, and some immigration. The Peace of Montreal on June 25, 1701 had concluded hostilities between the French and the First Nation peoples. The mounting friction between the French and English, both in Europe and in North America, had fortunately not really touched the small village.

Life seemed settled for them all, in Rivière-Ouelle at least, but as it turned out, only for a short time.

13

Jeanne alone 1703–1716

While isolated in its location far to the northeast of Quebec along the southern shore of the St. Lawrence, Rivière-Ouelle had not been spared deaths from epidemics. In 1688, nine people had died from smallpox and measles, and in 1699 the influenza that claimed the lives of Jeanne's husband Robert Lévesque and of her last Lecanteur son took nine other lives as well.

Four years later yet another epidemic, another round of smallpox, spread through New France. There were six deaths in Rivière-Ouelle between April 1703 and the end of that year. Among the dead was Jean-Baptiste-François Deschamps de la Bouteillerie. Jean-Baptiste died on the 16th of December, 1703 in Rivière Ouelle, a day before his brother Adrien died in France.

Headstone of Jean-Baptiste-François Deschamps

Jean-Baptiste was buried on December 16, 1703 underneath the seigneurial pew in the church in Rivière-Ouelle. There is no indication that any of his sons attended the service.

Today, the gravestone to his honor in the current cemetery marks the location of the seigneurial pew or somewhere close to it, based on recent archeological findings. It is very near the stone indicating the site of the first church.

Deschamps' gravestone does not date from his death. It replaced a wooden cross that was set there in August 1896 by "his descendants, F. D. Monk, Esquire (a member of Parliament), and Jean de Boishébert." Records for markers prior to 1896 or for the placement of the current gravestone are missing.

Deschamps' death was said to have been grieved throughout the seigneurie, in apparent testimony to his involvement in the community. As one of only two dozen French noblemen in 17th century New France, he may have arrived with a noble's presence and may have kept some of the vestiges of that status. He did after all have a seigneurial pew in the church, did receive payment of taxes and rents owed him, and was, it is believed, feted every year with a Maypole in front of his home. However, unlike many other nobles in Quebec at the time, a majority of whom apparently abandoned or left their land grants for others to manage in order to remain in their homes in Quebec City, Jean-Baptiste preferred to live alongside his habitants. He also appeared to lead a simpler life than other nobles who built stone manors on their seigneuries and ventured into other businesses to build their wealth. Instead there is some evidence that he was quite generous with his concessions, giving out fishing as well as hunting privileges, and lenient in the collections of rents.

Rivière-Ouelle had been his home for over thirty years, and he built a community of friends, habitants and relatives of his deceased wife both there and in surrounding villages. Since his wife's death, his sons had been living either in Quebec or France, where he still had family. During his lifetime, Jean-Baptiste had witnessed the entry into the priesthood of his oldest surviving son, Charles-Joseph, and seen the progress of his other two sons in the military.

Jeanne's married life with Jean-Baptiste had been short, only two and a half years. When he died, Jeanne was 60 years old. She had outlived three husbands, had buried six children, but still had three sons, one daughter-in-law, and one grandchild. She also now had a title and was referred to in documents and presumably among the people of Rivière-Ouelle as "Madame de la Bouteillerie." Again, as in 1699 after the death of her second husband, she chose to stay in Rivière-Ouelle.

On November 16, 1704, Jeanne's youngest son Joseph married Marie-Angélique Meneux, another Rivière-Ouelle resident who was seven years his senior. Seven months later, Pierre-Joachim married Angélique LeTarte, a daughter of Jeanne's old friends in L'Ange-Gardien. Jeanne most likely traveled to L'Ange-Gardien for the wedding which her other two sons also attended. Since she was surrounded by old friends, would her son's wedding have brought back memories of her own wedding with Robert? Did she have the time or inclination to reflect on her life over the past twenty-five years?

Now that all her sons were married and now that Jeanne was once again a widow, the family needed to come to a final, more permanent arrangement regarding the family's property and the care of Jeanne in her later years. The new agreement with her sons, signed on July 25, 1705, apparently finally ended some continuing tensions in the family that seemed to have persisted even after 1702. The new document confirmed the earlier arrangements but annulled the separate agreements she had made with François-Robert and Pierre-Joachim. She gave up the rights to the land that she held as Robert's widow and also to the piece of the Renaud property that she and Robert had given to Jeanne's son Charles. She did, however, keep the land that Deschamps had granted in 1689 to Nicolas, her oldest Lecanteur son.

As was the custom with other widows and aging parents at the time, arrangements were made for Jeanne's remaining years. She was to keep her personal belongings, including her bed, presumably that feather bed with the green tower, and to have her own room in the home of one of her sons. The sons promised to build a brick stove in her room and to each supply her annually with four cords of wood for heating. They agreed that every year they would each give her one fat male pig, 25 bushels of wheat, and 30 livres to purchase incidentals, such as clothes, wine and other necessary items. They agreed to "winter, shelter and milk a cow and feed a chicken and rooster for her benefit." She was able to keep 400 livres for prayers upon her death. She also kept seven bulls, although she lent two to each of two of her sons, but not François-Robert, to have the use of them for four years. They all agreed to care for her, should she become invalid and no longer able to care for herself. She stipulated that they could not rent out the room if she decided to live elsewhere for a time, apparently allowing herself some flexibility in her future plans.

Finally, they all agreed to consequences that included the return of his allotted portion by any son in the event he failed to comply with the agreement. They also agreed to meet any of Jeanne's additional needs not defined in the agreement, should they arise in the future.

Once she had consented to these arrangements, her sons, according to the document, went into another room to negotiate the details and decide on the final distribution of land. Pierre-Joachim received the family homestead and therefore agreed to make a home for Jeanne. François-Robert received the house, barn, and land from the Renaud purchase where he had been living with his family. The two older boys agreed to build a home, barn and stable for Joseph since his share did not include those buildings. After they arranged for the division of the rest of the property among themselves, the document was signed by the notary Janneau and witnesses. Jeanne and her sons provided their marks, instead of signatures.

Over the next eleven years, twenty-one more grandchildren would be added to her family. Jeanne attended at least some of their baptisms as well as those of other families in Rivière-Ouelle.

On June 20, 1711, with the consent of her three sons and in front of two witnesses, Jeanne sold the land along the St. Lawrence that Deschamps had granted to her son Nicolas to Jacques Blois. Once again, the document notes that Jeanne could not sign her name. It is not clear why she sold the land instead of keeping it for her sons. Perhaps they did not need any more land, especially land that was not cleared and was not contiguous with their property. Or perhaps it was part of a deal negotiated in exchange for some work or service Blois had provided since it appears that the price of 100 livres was waived instead of being paid.

In January, 1713, she had her will drawn up by the notary Janneau. Having settled any inheritance issues in 1705, Jeanne apparently wanted to make specific arrangements and some special bequests.

The will, an unusual action for women—and men—at the time, did follow a format prescribed in the formal notary's manual. After declaring herself to be a good Catholic and being of sound mind, she asked for her sins to be forgiven. She indicated she wanted a simple funeral to be held at the church in Rivière-Ouelle without any ceremony and at the least expense possible. She requested that any debts should be paid. She asked for masses to be said for her soul, for those of her now deceased sons from her first marriage, and for her second husband Robert Lévesque. She referenced the agreement executed in July 1705 that had settled her estate with her three surviving sons. She asked her "good friend" Etienne Bouchard to serve as Executor of her will. And she revoked any prior wills and codicils.

Regarding the 400 livres provided her in the 1705 agreement with her sons to be used for prayers upon her death, she identified specific amounts and the numbers of masses to be said at eight different churches. Among them were parishes in L'Ange-Gardien where she had lived and its neighboring villages of Château-Richer and Sainte-Anne-de-Beaupré. Also included were parishes in Rivière-Ouelle and surrounding settlements. The reasons for her bequest to the eighth parish, St. Michel in Sillery, remain a mystery that is still to be sorted out.

Apparently Jeanne had been able to accumulate another 400 livres from her yearly allowance because she left that amount, a not-insignificant sum at the time, to her god-daughter and first grand-child Marie-Jeanne Lévesque, possibly for having cared for Jeanne in her later years. She made no mention of her first or third husband, and in fact referred to Robert Lévesque as her "premier" husband, a word that can be translated as "first," "primary," or "main."

After writing down all of Jeanne's instructions, the notary Janneau then read the will back to her, a routine procedure at the time since she could not read or write. She asked for six words to be deleted as unnecessary or incorrect. These revisions included specifying the amount of money to be given to churches, clarifying the name of the executor of the will, and minor corrections that were crossed out in the original copy. Then the will was signed by Janneau and the two witnesses. Jeanne lived for nearly four more years, apparently leading an active life that included a possible attendance at a baptism in the village of L'Ange-Gardien on the north shore of the St. Lawrence where she had once lived, before the will went into effect.

Three months after Jeanne's will was written, the Treaty of Utrecht was signed in Europe, ending the War of Spanish Succession. In September of that year, two of Deschamps' sisters died within a day of each other. Two years later, on September 1, 1715, Louis XIV died in his palace at Versailles, at the age of 77.

On November 22, 1716, just over a year after the death of Louis XIV, on what must have been Jeanne's deathbed, her sons had the 1705 agreement confirmed in the presence of the notary. Two days later, on November 24, 1716, hopefully surrounded by her family, Jeanne died, two weeks after the birth of her twenty-third grandchild. She did not live to see the birth of another thirteen grandchildren or any great grand-children. By 1729, her descendants numbered close to fifty and continued to grow exponentially.

A large granite monument to Jeanne and her second husband, erected by the Lévesque Association, is prominently located near the entrance to the cemetery next to the church in Rivière-Ouelle. Although her birthdate is wrong, it is a fitting memorial to a founding mother and father of Quebec. It does not, however, mark the exact location of her grave. Wooden crosses that may have commemorated the original graves of Jeanne and Robert have long since disintegrated, unlike the stone markers of the same era that are so prevalent in New England. In addition, if Jeanne's actual grave is like those of the others who died around the same time, it has been moved at least twice as a result of the cemetery's relocations as Rivière-Ouelle grew. Her actual grave is now possibly located under the current church's parking lot, next to the cemetery.

Lévesque monument

Part Five

Legacies

Jeanne's legacy and the legacies of her three husbands

14

Jeanne's Legacy

In February 1717, three months after Jeanne's death, her sons gathered in Joseph's home and had the 1705 Agreement ratified. Unlike many other women at the time, Jeanne only had three surviving children, but the three of them, all of whom remained in Rivière-Ouelle for their whole lives, left thirty-two children who in turn produced hundreds of offspring. Jeanne's descendants include René Lévesque, the outspoken premier of Quebec and a leader of the Separatist movement, the American author Jack Kerouac, and of course the author's father.

None of Jeanne's sons followed their father into the carpentry profession. Her youngest son Joseph had married Angélique Meneux in 1704, the daughter of one of the first *Filles du Roi* to arrive in Quebec. Joseph and his wife appear to have worked hard to clear the land he had inherited and to purchase more land, with an eye toward taking care of their children. Joseph died in 1755, four years before his wife. They left behind nine children.

Her second son, Pierre-Joachim maintained the family homestead and took care of his mother until she died in 1716. Like his brother Joseph, he apparently was a hard worker and managed to provide well for his children. The inventory of his property took three days to complete. He and his wife Angélique LeTarte, who could sign her name, were survived by twelve children. Angélique died in 1742, and Pierre-Joachim lived for another seventeen years, before falling victim to typhus and dying just prior to the fall of Quebec City to the English in 1759.

François-Robert, her oldest son and the godson of Jean-Baptiste

Deschamps, lived until he was 85 years old. He and his wife Charlotte Aubert survived the destruction of Rivière-Ouelle by the British during their march to Quebec City. François-Robert and Charlotte Aubert had eleven surviving children, including Jean-Baptiste, the author's ancestor. Reflecting the small and close community in Rivière-Ouelle at the time, Jean-Baptiste married Marie-Josephte Bérubé, the granddaughter of Jeanne Savonnet, another *Fille du Roi,* and Damien Bérubé, Robert's friend and neighbor from France.

François-Robert started a pitch production factory in 1730. He probably benefited from the King's support of the pitch extraction industry and also from sales of land that his wife inherited from her parents. Apparently he had challenging relationships with his employees and neighbors, as well as with his brothers and mother, and shut down the business after less than two years in operation. His other entrepreneurial efforts included a fishing venture while he continued to farm the properties he had inherited from his parents. He died a few months after his wife in 1765.

When Marie-Jeanne received the bequest from her grandmother, she was eight days shy of her 14th birthday. Six years later, on August 31, 1722 she married Joseph Miville, the grandson of Rivière-Ouelle pioneers Jacques Miville and Catherine Baillon. The disposition of the 400 livres left to Marie-Jeanne by Jeanne was not referenced in their marriage contract, although there is mention of a cow that her grandmother had given her. Marie-Jeanne and Joseph had twelve children, with all but one surviving them. Joseph died on July 30, 1780. Marie-Jeanne lived on for two more years and died on April 20, 1782 in Rivière-Ouelle.

As for New France, despite initial efforts and investment, the colony's growth seemed to stall. Its future would be shaped by the King's economic policy, which hampered development of any manufacturing or non-agrarian endeavors, and the lack of attention and financial support because of distractions in Europe. In 1760 the 85,000 inhabitants of New France compared very unfavorably to the 1.2 million people living in the European colonies to the south.

Some historians would say that the borders of New France extended too far for the small population to protect, without significant help from the home country. Louis XIV's desire for power and aggrandizement in Europe would prove, in the opinion of many historians, to be short-sighted, at least as far as New France was concerned. The French reached the highest peak of expansion in North America in 1712 from Hudson Bay to Louisiana. But, a year later, in the Treaty of Utrecht that ended the war between England and France and their allies, France gave up significant pieces of her territory. Acadia became Nova Scotia and was once again returned to England. Newfoundland, at the mouth of the St. Lawrence, and Hudson Bay were also handed over to the English.

Over the next several decades, England continued to threaten France over its remaining possessions in North America. Quebec City was bombarded, besieged by the British, and defeated on the Plains of Abraham in 1759. Montreal and the rest of the colony fell the next year. Despite their position as the conquering nation, the British wanted to ensure that the French inhabitants in Canada did not become rebellious like their neighbors in the New England colonies to the south. In an attempt to avoid such problems, the British enacted the Quebec Act of 1774 that allowed French civil law to continue for private matters, while keeping English Common Law for community matters. The seigneurial system was retained. The act also allowed the French to continue to practice the Catholic faith. Their plan apparently succeeded. Despite having had their countryside ravaged by the British, the French did not respond to overtures from Benjamin Franklin who visited Montreal in the spring of 1776 in an attempt to convince the Quebec leaders to apply to be the 14th state in the union being formed to the south of Quebec.

After the American Revolution, many British loyalists fled to the upper areas of Canada. In 1791 the country was divided into Upper and Lower Canadas, but 50 years later, the Union Act united the two. The seigneurial system would survive until 1854 when the 250 remaining estates were formally dissolved. In 1867 when the Canadian Federation was formed, Quebec became one of its four provinces.

One hundred years later, in 1967 French President Charles De Gaulle visited Montreal during Expo 67 and from the balcony of the City Hall shouted "Vive le Québec Libre!" to much exuberant applause and loud cheers. The next year, René Lévesque, a very distant cousin of the author, initiated the separatist movement, the Parti Québécois.

It is tempting to wonder how Jeanne would have felt if she had been there to hear those somewhat controversial words, "Long live free Quebec!" Would she have been proud? Would she have taken some satisfaction in the achievements of her progeny in trying to sustain the heritage she and others had created? Would she have approved?

***

As for the author's family, her father's ancestors stayed in Rivière-Ouelle and its surrounding communities for five more generations. Her great great grandfather Martial Lévesque was part of the exodus of young men from Canada that occurred in the years from 1840 to 1930 when he brought his family to the United States. He joined other French Canadians from the same region in Quebec in settling in Nashua, New Hampshire. Unlike many who anglicized their names, Martial kept the name Levesque, although he dropped the accent mark. His children and their children all married French Canadian spouses. It was not until the next generation, that of the author's father, when any "intermarriage" occurred. In December, 1943, when her father married Judith Ann Hallstrom, a woman of Swedish and Scots-Irish descent, he became one of the first in his family to break the mold.

15

The Legacies of Jeanne's Three Husbands

Of course, Jeanne's history and legacy would not be complete without some mention of the legacies of her husbands.

Until the writing of this history of Jeanne Chevalier, not a great deal of attention has been paid to Jeanne's first husband, **Guillaume Lecanteur**. Although he left a trail of details and documents from his many land transactions and records about his sons and social life in L'Ange-Gardien, no single story about the man has emerged. The primary reason for this lack of attention or interest in his history is most likely attributable to his short life, his mysterious disappearance, and the premature deaths of his sons, who left no descendants.

In contrast to Lecanteur, much has been written about **Robert Lévesque**. Particularly in Quebec, the recent interest in unearthing the stories of the ancestors of the French Canadian nation is one major reason for the stories about Jeanne's second husband. There is thus a chapter devoted to Robert in the first of more than 25 volumes on the founding fathers of Quebec.

His most famous descendant is also responsible for a great deal of the attention. In 1980, Canadian biographers learned that René Lévesque, Quebec's then Premier, had an ancestor born in France. That discovery eventually prompted a visit by Lévesque to Hautot-Saint-Sulpice, Robert's birthplace. Not only did his visit generate interest in Robert's history, but his family story led the mayors of Rivière-Ouelle and Hautot-Saint-Sulpice to establish a "twin city" linkage. There is now a plaque, commemorating Lévesque's visit, installed in front of the town hall in

Hautot-Saint-Sulpice. In addition, an association has been formed there to welcome the growing number of Robert's descendants from Quebec and elsewhere seeking to find their roots. The association, working with Robert's descendants, has placed a statue of Robert in the church. Finally, there is now a book on Robert and at least two others on Robert and his family.

Statue of Robert Lévesque in Hautot-Saint-Sulpice

As is the case with Jeanne, there has not been a great deal of attention paid to **Jean-Baptiste-François Deschamps de la Bouteillerie**, her third husband—until recently. The reasons for his relative obscurity could include a lack of male descendants who bear his name in Quebec or the United States or perhaps his status as a nobleman. Thus his story is not included in the multi-volume series on Quebec's pioneers, although he is mentioned in a few of the stories and he is recognized in exhibits in Rivière-Ouelle.

In conjunction with the effort to recognize his contribution in the village where he was born, Cliponville, in Normandy, France, a story describing his life is now available on the website www.lynnelevesque.com. A slightly condensed version is included here.

Several challenges make it difficult to recreate his life and distinguish fact from fiction. Unfortunately, there are no detailed papers left from Deschamps' life in New France, other than the legal documents. There are no estate budgets or other accounting records and no journals in New France possibly because of the destruction of Rivière-Ouelle by the British during their conquest of Canada in 1759. The family archives in Normandy were also destroyed—by the Germans during World War II.

What remains are stories and a life pieced together by some diligent research. Such research has uncovered anecdotes about Deschamps that have no foundation in fact, stories told to either embellish or tarnish his legacy. One is that he was a member of the famous Carignan regiment sent over from France to Quebec in 1665. Since there is no record of Deschamps' participation in any of the regiments or any documented reference by Deschamps to a military background, this story has since been disproven. It's more than likely that the story developed because he had friends who had been in the military or because many of those individuals receiving grants in October 1672, when Deschamps received his grant, were military officers.

The other story comes from Asseline's reference to the grant Deschamps was supposedly expecting to receive in New France, somewhere between Montreal and Trois-Rivières. Again the story does not appear to factually based. There is no reference to such a grant in the archives in Quebec. This time the story seems to have been told to cast aspersions on Deschamps as a coward, since land to the west of Quebec City was said to be troubled with invasions from Amerindians. In fact, relative peace prevailed at the time, and all grants in that area were given to officers to secure the area for the future.

There are, of course, facts and then some conjectures about his life, as related earlier in this book. Deschamps died in December, 1703. He did not live long enough to learn that his second son died the next year in France, to see another son be named a canon of the cathedral in Quebec City in 1712, or to attend his youngest son's marriage. On December 10, 1721, eighteen years after his father's death, Henri-Louis signed a marriage contract with Louise-Geneviève de Ramezay, the daughter of the Governor of Montreal. The de Ramezay family could trace its roots in France back to 1532 and was a quite prominent family in early Quebec. The marriage contract ended with two pages of signatures of prominent individuals. The de Ramezay home still stands in Montreal as a museum.

Henri-Louis, who assumed the name of his French family "de Boishébert," and Louise had four children who survived them. Before he died in 1736, Henri-Louis had the family's noble status reconfirmed. Charles Deschamps de Boishébert, their fourth child, was born February 7, 1727 and entered the military at the age of fifteen.

Charles, the only surviving grandson of Jean-Baptiste-François Deschamps, went on to a distinguished career in a number of military campaigns in Acadia and elsewhere in Quebec against the Iroquois and the English. After the fall of New France to England in 1760, he moved to France, along with hundreds of other French families. There he first married his very distant cousin and then ended up spending eighteen months in the Bastille as a result of inquiries by the French government concerning the circumstances around the loss of the colony.

Upon acquittal of any wrongdoing and with money most likely earned from his military career, Charles purchased an estate in Raffetot, not far from the family's ancestral home in Cliponville. He became the town's mayor for a short time and managed to survive the French Revolution and the governmental changes that ensued and stayed active in the village. A roster of important municipal dates for the years 1788–1794 in Raffetot attest to his involvement in village affairs, although he did, of course, have to change his name from "Sieur," or "Lord," to "Citizen Deschamps."

Monument to Charles Deschamps

Charles died there on January 9, 1797. A marker in his memory, placed there by the "*Amitiés Acadiennes*," or Friends of Acadia, on June 16, 1991, sits in front of the town hall, next to the church.

Charles and his wife Charlotte-Elisabeth-Antoinette Deschamps had one son, named Roch Charles Gabriel Deschamps, born on June 18, 1762. This son married and had two children, a daughter and a son who died without children. Although women at the time kept their own name, children took on the name of their father. Therefore, Charles Deschamps' grand-daughter Henriette, who married into the prominent Letardieu family that still exists in France, did not leave descendants bearing the Deschamps de Boishébert name.

Thus, unlike Jeanne and Robert and many of their countrymen who went on to leave thousands of descendants in Canada and the United States, with the male line continuing for more than eleven generations, Jean-Baptiste's male line died out after only four. His granddaughters in Canada either joined the convent or married into the eminent Lanaudière and St. Ours families. Though they did not carry the Deschamps name, some of them did distinguish themselves through entrepreneurial or other business ventures. Family members with the Deschamps de Boishébert name live in France and are descendants of Jean-Baptiste's brother Adrien.

And what about the seigneurie that Jean-Baptiste-François Deschamps had worked so hard to build? His eldest son Charles-Joseph, as a canon of the cathedral in Quebec, gave up his rights to inherit the seigneurie for the sum of 4,000 livres in 1706. His brother Jean-Baptiste, who had died two years earlier in France, never married nor left any progeny.

Their brother Henri-Louis who had risen through the ranks in Quebec's military forces from Aide-Major at Quebec, to Captain in the Marine Corps, and then to Commandant at Detroit and Acadia, thus inherited the estate. He did not appear to play much of a role in Rivière-Ouelle after his father's death, other than collecting rents and spending 750 livres to have a mill built, until 1719. In that year, he petitioned for rights to establish a fishery along the St. Lawrence River. In his testimony in defense of his petition, he claimed that his father had spent 50,000 livres of his own money on the estate but that the estate was generating only 300 livres in revenue. The case was resolved in a compromise between de Boishébert and other interested inhabitants of Rivière Ouelle. The investment or revenue amounts have never been substantiated.

Rivière-Ouelle did not continue to grow as it had under his father's watch. Partly this was because only a small portion of land remained to be conceded as grants and partly because Henri-Louis was otherwise occupied. He did, however, replace the seigneurial manor in 1725. He also filed the required inventory of the estate, listing the inhabitants, their holdings and financial commitments and providing rich detail in land ownership. Generally, however, he was more occupied with his military career, which apparently paid him significantly more than the revenues from the estate.

When Henri-Louis died, at the age of 57, his widow inherited one-half of the estate and was "guardian of the minor children" for the other half of the estate. Louise de Ramezay managed to have a large piece of land added to the Rivière-Ouelle seigneurie in 1750, but decided to sell it fifteen years later. At her death in 1769, it was still not sold. Finally, nine years after it was put up for sale, the estate was sold to a family of merchants named Perrault for 36,000 livres by her son Charles who by then was living in France. Charles, according to one source, never set foot on the property. He argued that it was not making any money which is perhaps one reason why it took so long to sell.

Despite the relatively short lifespan of the life of Jean-Baptiste-François Deschamps de la Bouteillerie and that of his family and seigneurie, he did leave a legacy. When he arrived in Quebec, Intendant Talon mentioned how his arrival should give the King hope for the future of the colony. He appears to have been the type of nobleman, industrious and loyal to the King, that Talon wanted to attract to the colony. He has been called an "ideal seigneur" by historian Alain Laberge, an expert on Rivière-Ouelle's history. Deschamps also merited mention by Professor Cole Harris in his definitive history of the seigneurial system in early Canada. Harris specifically referred to Deschamps as an exception, compared to the majority of seigneurs, for bringing colonists to New France and for choosing to live on the land and take an active role in colonizing his grant.

As this history reveals, Deschamps deserves a great deal of credit for the founding and initial growth of Rivière-Ouelle. In fact, he was one of many early Quebecois "entrepreneurs." He chose to invest what appears to have been his inheritance in an enterprise in New France. He managed to convince eight men to join his venture and leave France with him in 1671. He paid for their passage to New France and three years of board and room there. He had to provide tools and supplies. He took on all the risk of possible failure.

And then after three years, he started to divide up his estate and make land grants, often generous ones, to those who had helped him get started. Until he died in 1703, Deschamps was occupied with his estate's development. He was able to slowly attract settlers to his land through grants and through their networks of friends from settlements closer to Quebec City. Some even arrived directly from France.

By financial measures, it does not appear that he enjoyed much success. While it is unlikely that he actually made an investment of 50,000 livres in the estate, as his son claimed, his efforts took money and he required additional financing. He had to take out loans, delay paying one man the amount he was due under his contract, and ask his family for any additional inheritance due him when his father died. His sons had to pay off his debts after his death. Given the problems the family had in trying to sell the estate, it probably was not all that profitable.

Perhaps he died too soon and left heirs who were preoccupied elsewhere. Professor Harris's analysis of any seigneurie's business model was that it needed to reach at least 50 families to really generate profits. Before Deschamps' death, there was almost that number of families on the property. He did attempt to expand and protect the activities of the seigneurie, but it appears that he never built a mill on his property as seigneurs were expected to do. Of course, building a mill was an expensive proposition. Sufficient demand or justification for a communal mill might not have existed until after his death.

Perhaps it was a lifestyle decision and he wanted to lead a less formal life. Once he gave his manor to the church, there is no evidence that he tried to rebuild one, but instead went to live in what must certainly have been a more humble abode than he could have had in France. He might have been content, knowing he had done his best to fulfill his promise to the King. In the process he had a more interesting, adventurous life than he would have had in France. His chosen lifestyle of moderation was a distinctly different one from that of other nobles who remained in Quebec or maintained grand social lives on their estates or who embarked on other careers, some of whom ended up in significant debt.

Whatever Deschamps' motivation, he did establish an estate that has grown into the municipality of Rivière-Ouelle. The town survived the devastation by the British in 1759. By 1790, close to 1,900 inhabitants were living in Rivière-Ouelle. The wooden chapel, first built in 1684 with Deschamps' help, has been replaced several times and is now a 19th century stone edifice. Descendants of the first colonists, including many of Jeanne's descendants, continue to reside there.

Rivière-Ouelle has evolved and changed over the centuries, but it still has much of its ambiance and history. For this, Jean-Baptiste-François Deschamps de la Bouteillerie, as its founder, deserves more recognition than he has received to date.

Conclusion

Jeanne's story does not end with this account of her third husband's life. There are too many questions still to be answered and leads to be pursued. No stone can be left unturned. Until then, however, acknowledgement of the contributions that she and other women like her have made cannot wait.

Jeanne's is not just a story about one remarkable woman, although it certainly is that. By sharing the details of one woman's life, without the embellishments of a romance novel, this history provides a different perspective on the lives of the *Filles du Roi* in New France. Like Jeanne, these resilient, adaptable women led lives of constant courage, dealing with the daily, exhausting effort of keeping themselves and their families going, to recreate a normal life in the midst of a strange, often tumultuous new world. Most were without family ties and frequently without close neighbors. They were clearly dealing with unchartered territory which they somehow managed to tame for themselves and their families.

They came with no written recipes or guidebooks since most could not read or write. Many were "city girls" like Jeanne who had known a very different life in France. They had to rely on their own wits and the help of their neighbors, priests, and friendly Amerindians to adapt what they did know to the challenges they found in New France.

It is, of course, true that they were—or at least proved to be—a select group of women: most of them strong, self-reliant, adventurous, and willing to take on these challenges in the hopes of a better life.

This situation was particularly true by 1671, when Jeanne arrived, as the program evolved and criteria for selection were tightened. And it is also true that these women had advantages over their peers in France once they arrived. New France provided good food and water, clean air, low population density, and a climate, that though harsh, did keep the population relatively free from disease. The colony enjoyed relative peace from the religious conflict, political upheavals and wars that prevailed in the British settlements to its south.

At the same time, of course, in New France, life was tough, hard, challenging, but in the end, for many, rewarding. When confronted with a climate unlike theirs at home, with strange foods, incredible dangers, wild animals, isolation, and frontier living, most of these women managed to survive. Although some did lose their lives, many of them, like Jeanne, thrived.

Jeanne's story also provides a glimpse into the details of life in New France in the last quarter of the 17th century into the first quarter of the eighteenth. Historian Laurel Thatcher Ulrich had access to letters, detailed court records, diaries and gravestones to write *Good Wives*, the story of women in the British colonies in the same period, Without that same store of detail or without a great deal of research, it is still possible to say that life in those years in New France for both women and men offered many choices and opportunities not found in the France of the *Ancien Regime.* Some settlers took advantage of these opportunities and others did not. One of the displays in the Museum of Civilization in Quebec City can be roughly translated to read: "All sorts of people—high-minded and low-minded, capable or not, came to Quebec. Some settled and some moved on. Not all were heroes, not all were rogues." It is also fair to add, "the deeper the research, the more profound the realization that they were, for the most part, men and women like Jeanne, ordinary enough but certainly courageous enough to make new lives for themselves and their families."

There are of course many missing details about the lives of these people. This history of the life of Jeanne Marguerite Chevalier touches, only tangentially and with a great deal of conjecture, upon relationships between the French immigrants and the First Nation peoples. These chapters leave out the destruction that was inflicted on these peoples in the process of settling the colony, a tragic story that others have more ably addressed.

Her story also only hints at the importance of creating new connections and building networks in the midst of so much isolation in the colony and the role that religion and Catholic priests, nuns and missionaries played as a connector of those communities and as a source of solace in times of grief. Certainly in small settlements like Rivière-Ouelle the community was tight-knit. Neighbors, visiting missionaries and priests must have provided support to one another. Families were formed from children marrying children of friends and neighbors. Rivière-Ouelle's growth was aided by the influx of families that Jeanne undoubtedly knew in L'Ange-Gardien and Château-Richer and probably encouraged to move to her new home where land was more plentiful and social barriers less rigid, at least as evidenced by Jeanne's and Robert's relationship with Deschamps. Jeanne's story thus begins to provide insight into life in a small community where, despite diverse origins, these men and women were able to work through different languages, laws, traditions, social classes, songs and stories to communicate and forge ties in their battle with the frontier.

There is still a lot to be learned about these and other social challenges and the ways the French colonists responded to them in New France in the late 17th and early 18th centuries. Little is known about how newly arrived men, like Jeanne's first husband Guillaume Lecanteur, made connections that later led to land deals and other business arrangements. How did he meet the men, from a variety of social classes, with whom he subsequently made deals? Nor is much known, in English to complement Lorraine Gadhoury's research in French, about upper class family connections, such as those Seigneur Deschamps had with the Couillard family, and how they played out in everyday life. Family connections did not seem to stop lawsuits! Hopefully, future research will provide more depth to all these themes.

Despite these limitations, Jeanne's story does provide more texture to the role that the *Filles du Roi* played in giving birth to a unique heritage. Along with the men who had found their way to New France, Jeanne and the other *Filles du Roi* helped create generations of French Canadians and a culture that has been handed down through the ages, and that now, some would say, is in danger of being lost. This culture is a special blend of the French regime that Louis XIV imposed on the colony and a mosaic of other influences. A loosely translated version of a sign from the Museum of Civilization in Quebec City describes this mélange best:

> The French had taken a long time to get their roots firmly planted in the North American continent. When the colony finally did take shape, after Louis and his ministers assumed control in 1663, it took on a form that was uniquely Quebec: a mix of French laws, administrative policies, and class structure along with the deeply rooted Catholic religion, all molded by Amerindian practices and culture, the forbidding climate, the vast distance back to the homeland of France, and the mix of very different French people who eventually came to live there. A melting pot of different institutions and attitudes and peoples of diverse origins, classes, and modest fortunes; the rigors of life; and influence of Amerindian peoples caused social distinctions to blur and changes made to the model to evolve into what is today Quebec.

The men, it is true, faced many dangers and suffered early deaths from accidents, illness, and from many years of hard work. Their political and economic endeavors have indeed been studied and received historical attention. However, it was the women, not just those founding fathers, who provided the glue that kept the various pieces together to create the French-Canadian culture. The women were, as Ulrich wrote in *Good Wives,* the center of the lives of their families, and their stories are the counterweight to the more frequently researched founding of commonwealths or development of ideas. Too little is still known, and may never be known because of the dearth of pertinent information, about the contributions of these *Filles du Roi* to the history and heritage of Quebec, although recent research and publications are signaling more interest and attention in this area.

In the midst of many unanswered questions and still to be researched themes, one fact is definitely known: Jeanne was the co-founder of a long line of descendants. To date, however, despite the fact that without Jeanne the many thousands of Lévesques and other descendants who share lineage back to Jeanne would never exist, she has not received the same recognition as her second husband Robert Lévesque. Currently there are no statues of Jeanne in churches and no memorial plaques, a situation that needs to be corrected.

Like many other *Filles du Roi,* Jeanne Marguerite Chevalier was an exceptional woman, "une femme formidable!" She faced many challenges, dangers and sorrows in her lifetime. She lost four of her children before the age of three and two sons before they could marry. Her relationship with her surviving sons, at least the oldest as far as is known, was a bit troubled, but she managed to resolve their differences and arrange for her care in her senior years. Jeanne and Robert made sure that their sons were provided for and that they married well.

From the pieces of her life that have been gathered together to date, it is safe to say that Jeanne was savvy, smart and practical. Jeanne was not necessarily different from any of the other 769 *Filles du Roi* in helping to create what is now Quebec, but her story does provide more detail on the choices and decisions one *Fille du Roi* had to make. To be sure, not all of her choices were smart ones. At the start of her life in New France, her first choice of a husband did not turn out to be the wisest. Fortunately, she apparently learned, or had the good luck, to make a better choice with Robert. And indeed her marriage to the third brought a somewhat fairy tale ending to her married life.

In all three marriages, from what is known, she was a helpmate, as well as a mother and wife. On her own she continued to be a wise and independent woman, friend and neighbor who lent money and was willing to forgive neighbors' debts. She made arrangements with her sons to ensure a comfortable future for them and for her own care as she aged. She ensured there were provisions for any eventualities should any of her sons not live up to their responsibilities and clauses to allow her flexibility about her own future. She saved money from the annual "allowance" she received from her sons and was thus able to leave an additional 400 livres to her goddaughter in her will. Finally, she wanted a simple funeral, "at the least expense possible."

Jeanne never learned to read or write or to sign her name, and apparently neither did her children, at least during her lifetime. But she did leave a precious gift to a long line of descendants. She left no gravestone, no diaries, no traces of herself behind, but she left a legacy for her descendants as a strong, determined woman. She created a life for herself and her children in the new world that she truly could not have imagined had she remained in France. She was a woman of action, strong will, and great courage.

Perhaps the complete history of Jeanne will never be known. There are so many gaps to be filled and mysteries to be solved. Nevertheless, her story, no matter how incomplete, must be kept alive for generations to come, to be shared with all her descendants so that she, and other women like her, receive the recognition and appreciation she deserves.

"The people we love will live on so long as we pledge to
tell and retell the stories of their lives."

~ Doris Kearns Goodwin,
April 25, 2014 in Boston

Epilogue

The history of Jeanne Marguerite Chevalier and her three husbands ends here—for now.

Keeping Jeanne's history alive and giving her the recognition she deserves has not been, nor will it be, an easy task. Despite increasing availability of records on the Internet and in archives in Quebec, France and the United States, challenges for the researcher are many.

First, when Jeanne left France in 1671, she was, as far as is known, an orphan from at least one parent; she came from, at best, a family of moderate means. For most people in those economic or social situations—basically, just ordinary, everyday people, there were no reasons for recognition, other than business transactions and normal life events, particularly in 17th century France. No Internet or other forms of social media kept the world or the community current. No diaries, journals, letters or other forms of written memoirs told the intimate details of their lives. For the most part, only key events, such as births, marriages and deaths, were registered in the most convenient neighboring village and parish, usually but not always those of the family. Any movement between villages and towns for work or family reasons make searches for documents even more difficult. No comprehensive database or even an index of records or information by region or for all of France has been organized, as it has been in Quebec. So searches must be conducted at local archives, village by village, a time-consuming effort even when approximate locations are known. That has been the struggle to find more information regarding Jeanne's parents.

In France, for sure, any documents that did exist at some point may have vanished. There have been fires, wars, and revolts in the centuries since 1643, including the French Revolution when many churches and their records were destroyed, and the raid on Dieppe in 1694. The Second World War also wreaked havoc on lives as well as the archives in Dieppe during the 1942 Canadian raid on that town. Similar destruction occurred in Saint-Lô and Coutances as the Allied forces landed on the beaches of Normandy over 70 years ago.

Amazingly, many of these documents do still exist and that actually leads to more complications. When a document or record, such as the acts of baptism for Lecanteur or Deschamps, cannot be found, it is impossible to figure out whether the event just never happened, was never registered because of the absence or unavailability of a priest or notary, or whether the document was lost because of human error, eaten by rats, damaged by the climate, or just misplaced.

Because there are mysteries yet to be solved and gaps that still need to be explored to determine if they can be filled in or just left as an unknown, the search for the details of Jeanne's life in France must and will continue, despite all of these frustrations. Uncovering Jeanne's story in Quebec has been somewhat less complicated—to a point. Existing documents in Quebec are much more numerous and easier to find, thanks to the *"Programme de recherche en démographie historique"* at the University of Montreal or PRDH, with its extraordinary index and database of 300,000 records, dating from the early 17th century. However, many challenges in Quebec are similar to those in France. Fewer documents might have been lost in fires or wars, but not all actions were documented, although an incredible number were preserved, leaving those same unanswered questions about their existence. In Quebec the possibility of verbal agreements, of which they are said to be many, adds another twist to research.

The whereabouts of Jeanne's third husband, Jean-Baptiste-François Deschamps de la Bouteillerie, during the years 1689-1692 are a revealing example of many of the challenges. Did he remain in Rivière-Ouelle during those years and just not make any grants or attend any baptisms or marriages? Was he perhaps ill and unable to attend any events? Were grants made, but just were not recorded? Or did he, as historian Paul-Henri Hudon suspects, return to France to visit with his family and bring them and the relatives of his countrymen news from Quebec?

Then there is the challenge of being able to read documents since any existing original deeds, records, contracts or other legal documents that can be unearthed—whether in France or Quebec—are in old French and handwritten by notaries and priests. Less than legible penmanship, ink smudges, and thin paper, where both sides were used for recording, complicate the research work. The documents are also old, torn and otherwise damaged through the ages, making them even harder to decipher. Some of these fortunately have been transcribed, at least in Quebec, but only a few. And the rest are to be read on often temperamental microfilm machines, not the easiest task!

Even if the documents are found and can be read and understood, there are still more challenges. The events were not always recorded on the day they occurred. Thus, accurate details were subject to the authors' memories, hearing, interpretations, and ability to keep good notes for later entries. In this day of omnipresent Internet access and a tablet in every pocket, it's hard to believe. Nevertheless, many events that occurred in countryside villages were often written on bits and scraps of paper by priests traveling between distant settlements, intended for later transfer to registers which may or may not have happened. According to one of the archivists in Quebec City, something like 20% of all life events were not even recorded—at least in Quebec—because of the absence or human error of a priest or a notary.

Those documents that do exist often contain inaccuracies around dates, missing dates of birth, misspellings of names and places, and errors made by notaries, mistaking one person for another. The confusion over Jeanne's mother's name is one good example. Jeanne's last name as well has been variously listed as "Jeanne Leroi" (in the record of her third son's baptism)," Le Chevalier," and "Chevalier" elsewhere. Since Jeanne probably could not read, like the majority of men and women at the time, she would not have been able to correct a priest or notary or other official in any of these cases!

Then there are misinterpretations by writers and historians, such as assuming that a reference to the parish of an individual's parents meant the place of baptism, instead of the place of last residence. In addition, writers, even highly respected historians, have been misled because they trusted only one source or because they relied on stories, often embellished, unsubstantiated, and conflicting, handed down through the years. The stories about Deschamps connection with the Carignan Regiment and about his original land grant are just two examples. Details can be overlooked, the context of the event, or perspective or actual knowledge of the author not considered. Triangulation, the goal of the historian to verify information from more than one source, in Jeanne's case is close to impossible.

Still, if I want to finish this first edition, I must rely on and trust the accuracy of reputable sources, such as historians Leslie Choquette, Cole Harris, Paul-Henri Hudon, Alain Laberge, Yves Landry, Renaud Lévesque, Ulric Lévesque, Peter Moogk, Jan Noel, Marcel Trudel and others, to translate, transcribe and interpret documents. I can trust these sources, with one caveat. Several works were written many decades ago. New material has appeared over the years. More documents have been published, and the Internet has made more information and connections available. Some of the more recent information contradicts earlier stories and clarifies misunderstandings.

Nevertheless, these authors have abilities and access that are beyond my timespan to acquire, particularly around the French language. After all, an obsession with perfection could seriously hinder completion of Jeanne's story!

All of these factors make resurrecting Jeanne's life in France and in Quebec quite a challenge. It involves researching archives, analyzing conflicting stories, and understanding the context of the times in which Jeanne's story unfolds. It necessitates a working knowledge of French to read and understand written material and to communicate with archivists. It entails piecing together uncovered details with live interviews in France, Quebec and the United States, and then adding some glue from reasoned hypotheses, based as much as possible on facts, with the added ingredient of some imagination, wisdom and hopefully inspiration from Jeanne. It also requires the ability to prioritize and analyze to figure out if a missing piece of information is really all that important!

Finally writing her story calls for a comfort level with probabilities, not certainties, as one author put it. Jeanne's story is thus part history and part detective story, or perhaps a new genre: conjectural history. Or, as respected archivist Renaud Lessard told me, "We cannot write history for those years. We can only write about the traces of history."

Then here is a personal preoccupation. It's not only been hard to uncover the details of Jeanne's life. I find it just as troubling to try to write about someone with no pictures, no journals or letters. Although I have a copy of her will which provides wonderful insight into her character, it was dictated and written down by a notary and followed a traditional format so her personal feelings were not recorded. Since she probably could not write, there are no letters that record her emotions around relationships with her husbands and her sons or around events that took place, such as birthdays, births, or deaths.

Therefore, I have to try to weave these details together from notarial records and from secondary sources, not an easy task when trying to truly understand her personality and character. From what I know about her life so far, I'd say she was tough, adventurous, resilient, quite intelligent, and financially savvy. But there is more that I want to know. Did she have manners and some sort of sophistication, despite little formal education? Did she ever get angry? Did she have a temper or was she like many women of the time at least in France: more patient and aware of her place? How did she deal with all the trials and tribulations around sudden disappearances, changes in fortunes, deaths both early and late? Did she cry often? What about her smile? Did she smile and laugh a lot? What did her voice sound like? What sort of dialect did she speak?

How tall was she? Judging from historical information, she

probably was not much taller than 5 feet! What color were her eyes? Did she have freckles? Was she thin, stocky, or somewhere in between? What were her hands like—as a peasant and then later as a lady? For some reason I feel compelled to visualize her, to hold a picture of her, at least in my mind. Yet, how can I do that since there are no pictures of her? The only likenesses are the peasant women in the Nain Brothers' paintings in the Louvre or scenes from the *Maison St. Gabriel* museum in Montreal dedicated to the *Filles du Roi*. To be sure, during the *Fête de la Nouvelle France* in Quebec City in August 2014, there were actors playing the parts of the *Filles du Roi*. They did in fact give me some idea of what she might have looked like. Her hair would have been bound by a kerchief or cap of some sort, and she would have been wearing a skirt with an apron that fell to mid-calf and clogs or *sabots* on her feet. In her later years, I picture her as somewhat more elegant, like Cary Grant's grandmother, in "An Affair to Remember:" a bit fragile and dressed in black with a lovely white lace shawl.

These conjectures, these guesses are really all I have. Just recently, I happened upon an article about another *Fille du Roi,* written by Suzanne Sommerville, like me a descendant of a *Fille du Roi*. At the end of her article, describing her ancestor and the *Filles du* Roi, she summarizes my quandary:

> Each of these women was an individual, with talents, faults, personal histories, and the full gamut of human emotions that women continue to feel today. They lived in a historical time that had customs of its own, with daunting space-and-time distances between France and New France: no telegraphs, telephones, or internet existed. Those of us who rely on documentation to tell their story can cite the surviving written records… but can we ever understand the feelings and personal motivations, the joys and regrets, the tragedies, with complete certainty. As Ken Kesey wrote: "I've never seen anybody really find the answer, but they think they have."

I am willing to admit—at this point anyway—that I have not found nor do I think I have found the answer.

The final challenge is that described by Peter Moogk, in his book *La Nouvelle France*, where he writes that the job of the historian is "to explain, in clear prose, how the present came into being," to enlarge "the reader's understanding of why things evolved as they did," and to provide "a credible interpretation [that] will appeal to the evidence and allow the reader to verify that there is a foundation for the writer's view." I still need to figure out what Jeanne's story means to my life and to the lives of my extended family. I feel as if I am only halfway there.

This task, this journey to find the traces of Jeanne, to give her the voice she deserves, and to find the meaning in her life, has not been easy. I am, however, determined to persevere—to fill in gaps, particularly in France, and to resolve mysteries regarding Jeanne's life and those of her three husbands. In the meantime, if readers have any alternative interpretations of my conjectures, any corrections to offer, and any contributions of information to fill in the blanks, please email me at lynnelevesque@gmail.com.

The journey to date, while challenging, has had many rewards not captured in this first edition of Jeanne's history. Along the way in this search to uncover the facts about Jeanne's life, I have had many extraordinary experiences and marvelous adventures and have met an amazing number of outstanding people. All of those stories and hopefully some more answers or some resolution to my questions are the subject of my next book on Jeanne!

Appendices

Cast of Characters

Many people played a significant role in Jeanne's life, some directly and some more tangentially:

There are three main characters (besides Jeanne, of course!). One of them is relatively well-known by his descendants in any case: **Robert Levesque, Jeanne's second husband** (1679-1699). He is, after all, the ancestor of René Levesque, Premier of Québec from 1974-1977 and primary architect of the Separatist movement in Québec. Because of this interest in him, there is already a book devoted to his life and a chapter in the first volume in a 28-volume set on Québec Pioneers, *Nos Ancêtres.*

The other two main characters are relatively unknown:

Jeanne's first husband, **Guillaume Lecanteur** (1671-1678). Information about Lecanteur is sparse. He does not merit a chapter in *Nos Ancêtres.* To date, there has been only a little research on him, probably because he left no descendants other than his sons who died before marrying and left no children.

Stories about **Jean Baptiste François Deschamps de la Bouteillerie**, Jeanne's third husband (1701-1703), appear in several books, as the seigneur and founder of Rivière-Ouelle, and in two monographs about his family. There is no chapter about him in the 28-volume set *Nos Ancêtres*, presumably because he also was not survived by male descendants in Canada or perhaps also because he was a nobleman. Deschamps was married to **Catherine-Gertrude Macart** from 1672 until 1681.

Then there are those who played a more tangential role in Jeanne's life:

Jacques Cartier: Explorer from St. Malo in Brittany who claimed New France in the name of King Francis I in 1534.

Samuel Champlain: French navigator, cartographer, and explorer from the west coast of France who founded Quebec in 1608. Often referred to as the "Father of New France."

Jean-Baptiste Colbert: Louis XIV's Minister of Finance, and the major architect of the decision to aggressively settle the colony of Quebec and of the *Filles du Roi* program.

Louis XIV: King of France from 1643 until 1715 and chief sponsor of the *Filles du Roi* program.

Louis de Buade, Comte de Frontenac et de Palluau ("Frontenac"): Governor General of New France from 1672 to 1682 and from 1689 to his death in 1698.

Jean Talon: Intendant of Québec from 1665 to 1668 and from 1670 to 1672, responsible for ensuring the *Filles du Roi* program was properly executed in Québec.

Others who appear throughout her life, including her three surviving sons, are described in the appropriate chapters.

Acknowledgements

I am blessed with an incredible family of friends and network of colleagues who have been and continue to be most supportive of my efforts in the saga of Jeanne and my search for the details of her life.

To date, these sometimes overlapping circles of friends, family and colleagues include the following deserve special mention: Kathi Barry Albertini, Ann Auburn, Edith Bédard, Jacques Deschamps de Boishébert, Nadine Lefebvre, Carol Lundquist, Helaine Simmonds, Arthur Strout, Seta Wehbe, my friends from Australia Theodora Noble and Susanne Dennings, my sister Carla Levesque, and my cousins Father Peter Dumont, Vivian Dumont, Susan Littlefield, Sister Marie-Cristilla (whom we also know as Muriel Pelletier) and Peter's cousin Michel Moisan. I owe very special thanks to Peter and Michel for helping with early translations and with brainstorming possible explanations to some of the mysteries around Jeanne and her family. In addition, although only a distant cousin, historian Ulric Lévesque not only has been willing to answer questions and provide promising hypotheses despite my halting French. He also took the time to give me a special tour of Rivière-Ouelle when I visited the village where Jeanne and Robert Lévesque lived centuries ago.

Several historians have been most responsive with emails and conversations, including Leslie Choquette (thanks for the lovely afternoon chat in your backyard!), Cole Harris, Paul-Henri Hudon, Alain Laberge, Yves Landry, Rénald Lessard, Renaud Lévesque (thank you so much for all your answers to my questions), Eric Mardoc, Peter Moogk, and Jan Noel, several of whom have had to reach back many decades into research done so long ago.

In Quebec and France, archivists at the following institutions have been amazingly helpful, and I am most appreciative of their aid in tracking down documents and information:

The staff at *Bibliothèque et Archives Nationales au Québec* (BANQ) in Montréal;

La Société Généalogique Canadienne-Française, especially Suzanne Galaise and her staff of volunteers;

BANQ Quebec at Laval University, particularly Rénald Lessard, Michel Simard, and Jean-Pierre Asseline;

La Société d'histoire de Charlesbourg, specifically René Cloutier and Cécile Labrecque;

Les Archives de la Côte-Du-Sud et du Collège de Sainte-Anne in La Pocatiere, Quebec, particularly Pierette Maurais and Michel Dumais;

Irène Belleau and Gérard Viaud, Société de l'histoire des filles du roy;

Veronique Goulle at *Les Archives Municipales de la Ville de Coutances* in France;

Bernard Quétel, Secrétaire, *Cercle de généalogie et d'histoire locale de Coutances et du Cotentin;*

The staff at the *Bibliothèque de Coutances;*

Louis Richer and Lise St-Hilaire at the Société de Généalogique Québécois;

Anne-Louise Lacourse and André Daviau at Société de généalogie de Longueuil, Quebec;

Guy Turquer, *Les Amys du Vieux Dieppe*;

The staff in France at the departmental archives in Rouen, Saint-Lô, Caen and in *le Fonds ancie*n in Dieppe's *Mediathéque.*

I also want to acknowledge the teachers and students in my writing seminars at Grub Street, Boston MA, and in my French classes with the Brookline Adult Education Department.

Of course, there are others whom I have fortuitously met along the way and who have encouraged me and provided contacts and incredible support. These include:

In Quebec: Edith Bédard, and Patricia Thomas in Quebec City; Louis-Georges Simard, Nancy Fortin, and Richard Dubé in Rivière-Ouelle; Micheline Parent, Hermance Lévesque Molnar, Fernand Lévesque, and other members of the Lévesque Association.

In France: Michel and Marie Bourdin, Brigitte Bernaudat, Arlette and Hervé Coutinho, Jacques Deschamps de Boishébert and his family, Béatrice and Alain-Paul Jolly, and Nadine Lefebvre in Dieppe; Jean-Pierre and Béatrice Levêque in Cliponville and Jean-François Lemesle, Mayor of Cliponville; Jean-Pierre and Dominique Eudier and Raymond Taconet in Le Havre; Jean Paul Monville, Mayor of Hautot-le-Vatois; and Nicole Gilbert, genealogist, and Yann l'Hostis in Granville. Much appreciation also to Ghislaine Cahard, President, and Nelly Mare-Godet of «Les Cousins du Nouveau Monde», for a delightful tour and luncheon in Hautot-Saint-Sulpice in 2015, and then the wonderful opportunity to speak in 2016.

In the United States, Sandra Goodwin for the interesting interview she conducted for "Maple Stars and Stripes: Your French-Canadian Genealogy Podcast."

I am fortunate to be living in the great city of Boston, with its incredibly rich resources for research. The New England Historic Genealogical Society and the staff there provided support, direction and access to innumerable resources in hard print and on microfilm. The Boston Public Library's Interlibrary Loan Department and particularly Kathy Kire in my local library have been diligent in following up on my many requests. Through them, I was also able to get access to Harvard University's unbelievable collection of historical resources.

I also must acknowledge the extraordinary work of Sylvia Tooker at Bear Data Services who created my website and blog and who has been friend and colleague for ever so many years!

I hope I have been able to remember the names of everyone who has helped me along the way, but if I have forgotten anyone, I apologize!

Glossary

One of the many challenges in writing this history of my 8th great grandmother Jeanne Chevalier is the use of French terms. Not every word has an exact translation into English, and often a translation can result in a loss of meaning. So I have chosen to use the French terms where it makes the most sense and have italicized them. I have tried to define them within the next sentence. Any translations are my own, unless otherwise noted.

There are also some English terms that need clarification! To help me in this task, I am relying heavily on Richard Colebrook Harris's book, *The Seigneurial System in Early Canada*. Although first written nearly 50 years ago, it is extremely helpful for many reasons, this task of translation or definition being just one of them!

Terms	***Definition / Translation***
Amerindians	This generic term refers to the First Nation peoples who inhabited Canada before the French arrived. I have only identified a particular group, such as Iroquois or Hurons, when appropriate.
Arpent	192 feet. A square arpent is 5/6ths of an acre.
Canada, Quebec New France	When Jeanne arrived in Quebec, the terms "Quebec," "Canada," and "New France" were used differently from their use today. New France (Nouvelle France) referred to the entire French colony in North America, which eventually at its height extended from Acadia (today Nova Scotia) west to Michigan and South to Louisiana, but excluding the Atlantic colonies. Canada was used for the colony's larger area along the St. Lawrence River, to differentiate from Acadia and Louisiana. However it was often used interchangeably with Quebec (Kebec). I have frequently used all three—New France, Canada and Quebec—interchangeably.
Censitaire	A settler on a seigneur's land who had certain obligations to the seigneur in the form of rents, days of service, and produce.
Domain	This term refers to the section of a grant set aside by the seigneur for his (or her rarely, but occasionally!) personal use.
Fief	A fief consisted of heritable property or rights granted by an overlord to a vassal who held it in return for feudal allegiance and service. See "seigneurie" below.

Terms	*Definition / Translation*
Filles du Roi	Daughters of the King. For more information about this program established by Louis XIV to colonize New France, see Chapter 2.
Habitant	A permanent resident of Canada operating a small farm.
League	Roughly 3 miles
Livre	A French unit of value, which can best be understood in relative terms. According to Harris, a laborer earned on average 2 livres a day, a skilled laborer up to five, royal officials of secondary rank from 300–3,000 livres a year, and the governor 12,000. A capon was worth about a livre. A sheep and pig around 10–20 livres, a cow 40–50 livres. Uncleared land was almost worthless, but a farm of average size with 20 cleared arpents (just under 20 acres), a one-room cabin, and a barn usually brought between 1,000– 2,000 livres
Rang	Within a seigneurial grant, land was arranged in rows, or "rangs." The first rang included land directly on the riverbank and was used for the initial grants to settlers. The remaining rangs were left for subsequent grants and further development of a seigneurie.
Seigneur	One of a group of individuals who held land directly from the king. In early years, seigneurs were people of nobility. In later years, the term was not necessarily indicative of noble rank. Since "lord" is a loaded word, I have used the term "seigneur."
Seigneurie	The land granted to a seigneur or the church, also known as a fief in France.

References

Armstrong, Sally. *The Nine Lives of Charlotte Taylor*. Toronto, 2008.

Beik, William. *A Social and Cultural History of Early Modern France*. Cambridge, 2009.

Bloch, Marc. *French Rural Society*, trans. By Janet Sondheimer. Berkeley CA, 1966.

Bouchard, René, ed. *La Vie Quotidienne au Québec*. Montréal, 1983.

Boucher, Pierre. *Histoire véritable et naturelle des moeurs et productions du pays de la Nouvelle-France vulgairement dite Canada*. Boucherville, 1964.

Bradbury, Bettina, ed. *Canadian Family History: Selected Readings*. Toronto, 2000.

Braudel, Fernand. *Civilization and Capitalism: 15th–18th Century. The Structures of Everyday Life: The Limits of the Possible*, Trans. Sian Reynolds. New York, 1981.

Briggs, Robin. *Early Modern France 1560-1715*. Oxford, 1998.

Brun, Josette. *Vie et mort du couple en Nouvelle-France*. Montréal, 2006.

Casgrain, Henri Raymond. *Les pionniers canadiens et le tableau de la Rivière-Ouelle; légendes*. Montréal, 1912.

Casgrain, Henri Raymond. *Une paroisse Canadienne au 17ème siècle*. Québec,1880.

Charbonneau, Hubert et al. *The First French Canadians: Pioneers in the St. Lawrence Valley*. Newark NJ and London, 1993.

Choquette, Leslie. *Frenchmen into Peasants*. Cambridge MA, 1997.

Christie, Nancy and Michael Gauvreau, eds. *Mapping the Margins: The Family and Social Discipline in Canada, 1700-1975*. Montreal and Kingston, 2004.

Couillard-Després, Azarie. *La première famille française au Canada, ses alliés et ses descendants*. Montréal, 1906.

Croff, Mme. E. *Nos ancêtres à la Rivière-Ouelle*. Montréal, 1931.

Dallemagne-Cookson, Elise. *Marie Grandin*. Philadelphia, 2003.

Desjardins, Sergine. *Marie Major : Roman historique de la vie d'une fille du roi*. Laval Québec, 2006.

Dickinson, John and Brian Young. *A Short History of Quebec*. Montreal and Kingston, 2001.

Douville, Raymond and Jacques Casanova. *Daily Life in Early Canada,* translated by Carola Congreve. New York, 1968.

Duby, Georges, and Robert Madrou. *A History of French Civilization.* New York, 1964.

Duchêne, Louise. *Habitants and Merchants in Seventeenth Century Montreal.* Montréal, 1992.

Dumas, Silvio. *Les Filles du Roi en Nouvelle France: Etude historique avec répertoire biographique, Cahiers d'histoire, no. 24.* Québec, 1972.

Eccles, W.J. *The Canadian Frontier 1534-1760.* Albuquerque NM, 1983.

Faillon, Etienne, Michel. *Histoire de la colonie francaise en Canada*, Vol III. Villemarie, 1866.

Gadoury, Lorraine. *La noblesse de Nouvelle-France: familles et alliances.* LaSalle Québec, 1991.

Gagné, Peter. *King's Daughters and Founding Mothers,* Vols I and II. n.p,. 2004.

Gariépy, Raymond. *Le Village du Château-Richer (1640-1870).* Québec, 1969.

Gariépy, Raymond. *Les terres de L'Ange-Gardien, Côte-de-Beaupré.* Sainte-Foy Québec, 2004.

Gaudu, Fernand. « Jean Deschamps des Landes et sa famille, XVIIe et XVIIIe siècles. » Unpublished manuscript. Caen, 1978.

Gauthier-Larouche, Georges. «Évolution de la maison rurale traditionnelle dans la région de Québec» (étude ethnographique). Québec, 1974.

Goubert, Pierre. *The French Peasantry in the Seventeenth Century,* trans. by Ian Patterson. Cambridge, 1986.

Goubert, Pierre. *Louis XIV and Twenty Million Frenchmen,* trans by Anne Carter. New York, 1972.

Goubert, Pierre. *The Ancien Regime. French Society 1600-1750,* trans by Steve Cox. New York, 1973.

Goujard, Philippe. *La Normandie aux XVIe et XVIIe Siècles.* Rennes, 2002.

Greer, Allan. *The People of New France.* Toronto, 1997.

Greer, Allan. *Peasant, Lord, and Merchant.* Toronto, 1985.

Grenier, Benoit. *Seigneurs Campagnards de la Nouvelle France.* Rennes, 2006.

Harris, Richard Colebrook. *The Seigneurial System in Early Canada.* Montreal and Kingston, 1966.

Hébert, Anne. *The First Garden* trans. by Sheila Fischman. Toronto, 1990.

Hudon, Paul-Henri. *Riviere Ouelle de la Bouteillerie, 3 siècles de vie.* Rivière-Ouelle, 1972.

Hudon, Paul-Henri. « Attaque de Phips sur Québec—300 ans. » *L'Estuaire généalogique.* Mai, 1990 pp. 770-779.

Laberge, Alain (ed.). *Histoire de la Cote du Sud.* Québec, 1993.

Laberge, Alain. « Seigneur, censitaires et paysage rural : le papier-terrier de la seigneurie de la Rivière-Ouelle de 1771, » *Revue d'histoire de l'Amérique française,* Volume 44, numéro 4, printemps 1991, p. 567-587.

Laberge, Alain. « État, entrepreneurs, habitants et monopole : le 'privilège' de la pêche au marsouin dans le Bas Saint-Laurent 1700-1730. » *Revue d'histoire de l'Amérique française,* vol. 37, n° 4, 1984, p. 543-556.

Lanctôt, Gustave. *Fille de joie ou filles du roi.* Montréal, 1952.

Lanctôt, Gustave. *A History of Canada,* Vol 2. Cambridge MA, 1964.

Landry, Yves. *Les Filles du roi au XVII Siècle.* Montréal, 1992.

Langlois, Michel. *Dictionnaire biographique des ancêtres québécois (1608-1700)* 4 vols. Sillery Québec, 1998-2001.

Lebel, Gérard. « Robert Lévesque « in *Nos Ancêtres,* Vol. 1, pp. 99-105. Sainte-Anne-de-Beaupré, 1993.

Les Premiers Français au Québec, sous la direction de Gilbert Pilleule. Paris, 2008.

Le Tenneur, René. *Les Normands et les origines du canada français.* Coutances,1973.

Le Texier, René. *Coutances histoire et description.* Coutances, 1973.

Lettres de Marie de l'Incarnation, par L'Abbe Richardeau. Paris, 1876.

Lévesque, Renaud. *Les Levesque de Hautot-Saint-Sulpice à Sayabec.* Montréal, 2006.

Lévesque, Renaud. *Robert Levesque et sa famille se racontent.* Levis, 2009.

Lévesque, Ulric. *325 ans... Une grande famille : Rivière-Ouelle vous accueille, 1672-1997.* Rivière-Ouelle,1997.

Lévesque, Ulric. *Robert Lévesque and His Era, trans. by Don Levesque.* Fredericton, N.B., 1999.

Lewis, W.H. *The Splendid Century.* Prospect Heights IL, 1997.

Mardoc, Eric. *Aventuriers Hauts-Normands en Nouvelle-France.* Hautot-Saint-Sulpice, 2007.

Mardoc, Eric. *Aventuriers Haut-Normands et Québécois.* Bonsecours, 2006.

Marie de l'Incarnation, *Word from New France : the selected letters of Marie de l'Incarnation.* Edited by Joyce Marshall. Toronto, 1967.

McNelley, Susan. *Helene's World.* n.p., 2014.

Mémoire de L'intendant Talon sur le Canada au ministre Colbert, Québec, 10 novembre 1670, dans *Rapport de L'archiviste de la province de Québec (RAPQ),* 1930-1, p. 125.

Mémoire de L'intendant Talon sur le Canada au ministre Colbert, Québec, 2 novembre 1671, dans *Rapport de L'archiviste de la province de Québec* (RAPQ).

Michaud, Adolphe. *Généalogie des familles de la Rivière-Ouelle: depuis l'origine de la paroisse jusqu'à nos jours.* Québec, 1908.

Mongrédien, Georges. *La Vie Quotidienne sous Louis XIV.* Paris, 1948.

Moogk, Peter. *La Nouvelle France: The Making of French Canada—A Cultural History.* East Lansing MI, 2000.

Moogk, Peter. *Building a Home in Quebec.* East Lansing MI, 2000.

Noel, Jan. *Along a River: The First French Canadian Women.* Toronto, 2013.

Ouellet, Fernand. «Propriété seigneuriale et groups sociaux dans la vallée du Saint-Laurent (1663-1840).» in *Mélanges d'histoire du Canada français offerts au professeur Marcel Trudel,* pp. 183-213. Ottawa, *1978.*

Ouimet, Raymond and Nicole Mauger. *Catherine de Baillon; Enquête sur une fille du roi.* Québec, 2001.

Parker, Geoffrey. *Global Crisis.* New Haven CT, 2013.

Parr, Joy ed. *Childhood and Family in Canadian History.* Toronto, 1982.

Quebec Women A History, trans by Roger Gannon and Rosalind Gill, ed. by The Clio Collective. Toronto, 1987.

Quénault, Léopold. *Recherches Archéologiques, Historiques et Statistiques sur la ville de Coutances.* Coutances,1862.

Rivière-Ouelle, Terre d'accueil depuis 1672. Rivière-Ouelle, 2014.

Roy, Pierre Georges. *La Famille Deschamps de Boishébert.* Levis, 1906.

Roy, Pierre Georges. *La Famille De Ramezay.* Levis, 1910.

Runyan, Aimie. *Daughters of the King and Founders of a Nation: Les Filles du Roi in New France.* Master's Thesis, University of North Texas, 2010.

Société d'histoire des Filles du Roy. « Colloque sur les Filles du Roy. Mères de la Nation Québécoise ». (CD and DVD) Québec, 2009.

Société d'histoire des Filles du Roy. « Hommage aux Mères de la Nation ». (Un coffret multimédia) Québec, 2016.

Sommerville, Suzanne. « Marie Claude Chamois, Fille du Roi, Wife of François Frigon: A Mystery » *Michigan's Habitant Heritage,* Vol. 34, #3, July 2013.

Sulte, Benjamin. *Histoire des Canadiens—Français, 1608-1880* Vol 4. Montréal, 1977.

Trudel, Marcel. *Histoire de la Nouvelle-France. Vol III. La seigneurie des Cent-Associés 1627-1663.* Montréal, 1979.

Trudel, Marcel. *Histoire de la Nouvelle-France.* Vol IV. *La seigneurie de la Compagnie des Indes occidentales, 1663–1674.* Montréal, 1997.

Trudel, Marcel. *Introduction to New France,* Toronto and Montreal, 1968.

Trudel, Marcel. *Les Débuts du Régime Seigneurial.* Montréal, 1979.

Trudel, Marcel. *The Beginnings of New France 1524-1663,* trans. by Patricia Caxton, Toronto, 1993.

Trudel, Marcel. *Les Ecolières des Ursulines de Québec 1639-1686.* Montréal, 1999.

Trudel, Marcel. *Le terrier du Saint-Laurent en 1674* 2 vols. Montréal, 1998.

Ulrich, Laurel Thatcher. *Good Wives.* New York, 1991.

Vaillancourt, Emile. *La conquête du Canada par les Normands, biographie de la première génération normande du Canada.* Montréal, 1930

Author's Biography

Lynne's life has been a constant process of embarking on new ventures and enjoying many learning experiences. She then somehow manages to rearrange these various pieces of her life in a multitude of different ways, almost like a kaleidoscope.

Although half French Canadian by heritage, she was raised in a non-French speaking home. She went off to college with four years of high school French, but decided to start a new language. Her degree in Russian Studies from Mount Holyoke College led her into teaching and then to graduate school at Rutgers University where she earned a Master's degree in Modern European History. Her love for history, particularly women in history, and for the French and Russian languages was, however, back-burnered by a 17-year business career (MBA from University of California at Berkeley) at two very large financial institutions.

In the middle of that career, a curious chain of events significantly readjusted the course of her life for the next 20 years when she rather serendipitously fell into the study of creativity. After completing her Ed.D at the University of Massachusetts, Amherst, she let her passion for the topics of creativity and leadership drive her departure from her banking career toward independent consulting and adjunct teaching positions in local colleges and universities. As part of that consulting practice, Lynne published *Breakthrough Creativity: Achieving Top Performance Using the Eight Creative Talents* (2001) and *The Breakthrough Creativity Profile and Facilitator's Guide* (2003, 2012), along with several articles on the topics of creativity and leadership. While still consulting, she spent 5-1/2 years as a senior researcher at Harvard Business School, where she co-authored multiple cases and articles on critical leadership challenges. Continuing to pursue more writing projects, she helped a dear friend write and publish his memoir *You Can't Win If You Don't Play* (2012).

Another set of unexpected occurrences led her to start on a different path while still working as a consultant. For over a decade now, she has been researching the history of her eighth great grandmother. The journey to uncover her ancestor's story has caused Lynne to come almost full circle back to her French Canadian roots and her love of history, although now more enriched by life's twists and turns. And after teaching, writing and talking about creativity for so many years and urging others to unleash their creative talents, she has now begun to access in depth all of her own talents as a dedicated writer of non-fiction.

Printed in Great Britain
by Amazon

54462325R00106